"We just can't do it here"

"So we need to open a Free School then"

"Okay... I'm in"

There was no risk.

The risk was carrying on doing what we were doing before.

That would have destroyed us.

We had no choice.

We had to do it.

You can do it, too.

Chapters

NOW!

(WELL... 2019...)

XP

XP is a school in Doncaster, UK.

It's an 11 to 19 mainstream academy which was opened through the Free Schools programme by two local educators, Andy Sprakes and Gwyn ap Harri.

It opened in 2014, taking in one year group at a time. Each year group has 50 students. XP will be full in 2021 with 350 students across 7 year groups.

XP was replicated in XP East, a second school based on the same principles and built right next to the original school, to form a campus which opened in 2017.

XP and XP East were joined by an existing local primary school, Green Top, in 2017 to form the XP School Trust, a multi-academy trust (MAT).

XP was created after visits to High Tech High and Expeditionary Learning schools in the USA left the founders with a moral imperative to create similar provision in their hometown of Doncaster.

The curriculum is delivered through 'Learning Expeditions' – academically-rigorous, cross-subject projects which result in students creating purposeful and authentic products which often exist outside of school, within the local community.

The school focuses on character growth and beautiful work, and as a result, students make outstanding academic progress.

In the local context, the school has a broadly average demographic through a borough-wide random lottery process for admissions, and has the highest attendance and lowest exclusion rate in Doncaster.

This year, in 2019, XP is eleven times over subscribed, with 551 applications for 50 places.

Teacher attendance is +99%. The school has never had to use a supply teacher. No full-time teacher has left.

In 2017, XP was judged by Ofsted to be outstanding in all areas.

The school is not yet fully formed, and it is far from perfect.

Perfect is overrated.

The school they couldn't kill

News 15 January 2010[1]
**Gwyn ap Harri tells the remarkable story of
Campsmount Technology College and Web 2.0**

It's Thursday January 7, 2010, the first day back at school after Christmas. Kids with coats on, stood in a small hall, huddled together like penguins, chattering then silent as our head welcomes them back with very proud eyes, warning them of the hardships they will face, but offering hope and expected success.

Today, thousands of schools across the UK are closed because of the snow. Today, we have 90% attendance, which is only more remarkable when we don't have a school.

You see our school, Campsmount Technology College, a medium-sized secondary school near the ex-mining town of Askern, north of Doncaster, burnt down in the early hours of Sunday, December 13. Apart from the new sports hall and a small building away from the main site, there is nothing left but burnt brick, ash and twisted steel. A sign hinged ironically over the front doors, half burnt but still legible says, 'Welcome to Campsmount'.

I got the call Sunday morning. I thought it was a joke. Travelling back from London, I realised we had no means of communicating with the students, parents or wider community. No post box, no telephone number, no kids' addresses, our servers and VLE which hosted our website, were all inside the building. All gone.

We knew what everyone would want to know; Will we get a new school? Will we have to go to different schools? What about our coursework? What happens now? What about our exams? And, of course, how did it start? Did a pupil do it?

---

1 While I was doing my NPQH, working with Andy at Campsmount, the school burnt down. I wrote an article about its resurrection and how we used technology to do this effectively. But ultimately, it was about the nature of school itself. The article was originally published on a website run by Merlin John.

We knew the fire would be covered by the local media, and these issues would fuel their frenzy for a good story. We needed to not only answer these questions, but take control of the communication that would inevitably ensue.

By Sunday afternoon, we had a Wordpress blog up and running under a web address set up a few weeks prior to host our Google apps. www.ctcmail.net would be our lifeline to hang all official announcements off. But how were we going to get this pretty random website out to the community?

We set up a Facebook group, official Campsmount fire updates (there was already an unofficial one even before we set ours up). By Monday morning, there were more than 1,500 members, and we started pushing out information through this and our new twitter account.

We needed to be really visible, so on Monday morning Andy Sprakes, our head, did a YouTube video which got more than 3,000 views. By the time the BBC and ITV came round with their cameras, I half-joked with the journalists that we didn't really need them.

We got the commitment to a new school pretty quickly, but even before then we had decided we must still teach our kids within the community, and ran around finding enough spaces in the local community to put together a makeshift school. A youth centre, a town hall, a local business park, and a couple of portacabins later we had a timetable and enough venues to give our kids at least half a day per year.

Unbelievably, we had sixth form lessons going within a day. The rest of the school only missed eight whole days, and it would have been seven if it wasn't for the snow.

We'd set up a laptop appeal – *'Be a PAL of Campsmount and Pledge a Laptop'* – where we asked organisations for one decent laptop. Not 10 rubbish ones, just one decent one. By the second week back, we had more than 100 laptops which meant we could teach ICT for all the timetabled classes. All were pledged from schools nationwide, the SSAT, the co-operative, and a surprising number of local businesses – despite the recession. We'd also asked for any resources anyone could spare – textbooks, paper, pens etc.

By the first week back, for some subjects, although old and battered, we had more text books than we had previously.

All this was conducted through our new Web 2.0 friends which has and still will work fantastically for us. Stuff like bus timetables were painlessly distributed by firing up Google Docs and linking it to our blog. The exam timetable went into Google spreadsheets.

We had no choice, but it's very brave using open internet technologies like this, where anyone can make comments using any kind of language, but look for yourselves, the hundreds of massively positive comments by students, teachers, parents and ex-students. In fact, I only saw three silly comments, and one of those was by an adult complaining about the standard of English being used in the comments. Go figure.

This was great, but it's not the whole story. That started the Friday before we were meant to break up for Christmas when we all got together at the Askern Miners Welfare centre. I've heard lots of stories where people say, "The community has really pulled together", but for Campsmount this was utterly true, and something that moves me every time I think about it.

Kids had come in to the Town Hall with the contents of their piggy banks. Old ladies, chattering about how they found out about it from Facebook, bringing in reams of paper and felt-tipped pens. A local sports kit provider printed 150 t-shirts from our design, *'We are Campsmount',* and we sold them all in under an hour. Bag-packing at the local Asda, arranged over the internet. Kids still being able to provide hampers to the old folk. The captain of Championship side Doncaster Rovers turning up for a fundraising football match. This all happened in the first week after the disaster happened.

On Friday December 18, the day we were meant to break up for Christmas. We had arranged a get-together in the local miners welfare. No one was expected to turn up. The kids had effectively got an extra week off at Christmas. All we had to offer were a few sweets, some soft drinks, *'We are Campsmount'* t-shirts and a copy of SingStar. It was jam packed with kids and teachers alike, and one of the proudest moments of my life. Kids were singing their hearts out, jumping around, revelling in their optimism and strength of community. I never thought I'd ever

say this, but Askern Miners Welfare, on that Friday afternoon... there was no other place in the world I'd rather have been.

To end it all, Andy addressed the buzzing crowd, and there was nothing more poignant and accurate said than when he explained to the kids that bricks and mortar don't make a school – we do.

It's not the buildings, the ICT, the organisation or processes. They can all help, but it's people that make a school exist and work. We didn't have any infrastructure left, but we all knew we still had a school.

Yes, we used the ICT around us to spectacular and instant results, but it's not about that. It's definitely not about pontificating about the amazing potential of geo-tagging, mobile and games-based learning whatever... whatever. Other people can carry on prancing around about that. Christmas has come and gone, and after the emotional roller coaster, we are all faced with the extremely hard task of getting some teaching done, and getting our kids through their exams in our makeshift classrooms.

Some things I know are true. We won't let the kids down and they won't let themselves down. And we will build the world class school that our community deserves.

We will do this because WE ARE CAMPSMOUNT!

Andy

This difficult period of time really consolidated my belief that a positive culture is the most important factor in making a school successful.

Like Gwyn, I was humbled by the power of community. It was only once we lost the school that I realised how important the school was to the community, the school wasn't just a 'place' but an intrinsic part of the fabric of that community.

I heard of how Year 11 students had broken down and cried when they heard the news, not tears of joy as you might expect but of genuine grief. I heard, saw and felt directly the swell of community support for the school. For example, I can remember countless acts of selfless kindness and support as we operated out of the Town Council Offices as we attempted to construct a plan to provide an education for our students. These acts ranged from donations of paper, pens, exercise books, laptops, furniture, provisions to keep us going and ad hoc collections of money from people who were not living in the most affluent of situations. It was both heartbreaking and uplifting and I will never forget the generosity of spirit shown by the community.

Andy

It instilled a feeling of responsibility and invincibility. With such support how could we not get the school back up and running, with such support how could we fail?

I could go on for ages about the impact the fire had and some of the strange, courageous and honourable ways that staff responded but the most important thing for me was that with a strong culture, strong relationships with stakeholders and strong community support you can do and achieve anything.

By the way, we didn't get the 'commitment to the school pretty quickly'. It was a real struggle both locally and nationally as the LA wouldn't make a commitment to rebuilding the school and any funding that we could have drawn down from Doncaster's ill-fated 'Building Schools for the Future' programme was axed by the Conservative Education Secretary, Michael Gove, when there was a change in government in the general election in 2010. We were left in limbo with no school and no plan to build another.

After many sleepless nights and many stressful days we finally managed, with support from the Local Authority, to negotiate with the Department for Education to access the funding for a new school.

It was fantastic news for students, staff and the community.

And well deserved, too!

www.bbc.co.uk/news/uk-england-south-yorkshire-11384769

TWO YEARS LATER...

Andy

So, two years on, we had survived a devastating fire, we had achieved an incredible Ofsted Report whilst struggling in portakabins during one of the most horrendous winters on record, and we had eventually built a new school. Then the phone rang...

Gwyn (breathlessly)...
"Hi Andy, you won't believe it but I'm in a school that... it's not part of the jigsaw... it is the jigsaw!"

Andy (skeptically)...
"Okay..."

Gwyn (still breathlessly)...
"Honestly, this is the answer. You have to see it."

Andy (still skeptically)...
"Okay. Gwyn, where are you?"

Gwyn...
"I'm in San Diego."

High in San Diego

"Do you mind if I tag along?"

When I asked my friend, Mark Lovatt, this innocent question, I didn't know it was going to change my life as much as it did.

I'd heard about High Tech High (HTH) from my friends Martin Said and Darren Mead, who had visited the school in San Diego through the Musical Futures programme.

I knew a few things:
1 It did project-based learning, which I thought was interesting.
2 It was in San Diego.
3 It was in San Diego.

I'd never been to America. I grew up in the 70s idolising everything USA, then I grew up in the 80s hating everything USA. I almost never even went because I got a horrendous cold and I'd asked my colleague, Simon Brown if he wanted to go instead of me. It was too late to change the tickets, so I bravely drugged myself up on ibuprofen and paracetamol and faced the journey myself.

I remember being in the airport, a bit disorientated, listening to everyone speaking in American accents and thinking they were all just putting them on. *"Hey you guys, move along up the hall. We've a whole bunch of y'all to get through customs"*. Then I imagined they took a fag break, and started talking in normal yorkshire accents. *"Ey up Rita. Ya gorra light, love?"*

At HTH, we met Laura McBain and Ben Daley. They said their school was based on design principles. I sniggered as I have a design background and know what design principles are and a school would never be based on design principles. Come on !?! Then I spent the next two hours wandering around this amazing school, and seeing their design principles manifest in the student work and the teaching practice.

We had three days at HTH, but after two hours, I just wanted to go to a bar and get drunk. My mind had exploded.

Our visit to HTH in San Diego.
Beautiful, inspirational work and curation.

While my colleagues were interested in how the timetable was structured, I'm saying to them, *"You're asking the wrong questions – they don't have the same problems as us."*

When I met Larry Rosenstock, all I could say was a feeble, *"thank you"* and I shook his hand, trying my hardest not to burst into tears. Luckily, they started talking about golf, which I hate, so it sobered me up from the brink, and I held myself together.

That evening, I remember saying to Mark over an IPA or two, *"Well, I either have to move to San Diego and work at HTH, or I have to work with a school to do this".* Mark, probably wisely said, *"You won't be able to do this in an existing school in the UK",* and I replied defiantly, *"Well I'll start a Free School then"...* to which there was a lot of laughter. The new government policy was seen as a joke by most teachers, including me.

When I got home I immediately did two things. I told Andy Sprakes he needed to go and see HTH (I figured he was more cynical than me, and maybe I was under some kind of illusion as to how good HTH was). I also ordered a book from Amazon called *'An Ethic of Excellence'.* Jeff Robin, the art teacher told me about a guy called Ron Berger, and that I should find out about him.

Surprisingly, Andy took me seriously and sorted a trip out pretty quickly with his Assistant Head, Jamie Portman. Simon Brown finally got the chance to go, too. On their return, and surprisingly, again, Andy was as convinced as me. He, Jamie and I arranged weekly meetings to come up with an implementation plan to transform his school, Campsmount, into a Project-Based Learning (PBL) school.

How Gwyn met Andy...

I'd left full-time teaching in 2004 to start my ed-tech company, realsmart. It was in 2010 when my company was working with the Specialist Schools and Academies Trust (SSAT), and during an evening meal at a conference at Arsenal football club's stadium, I randomly sat next to a guy called Pete and we realised we lived only a few miles from each other and even frequented the same pubs. I told Pete I wanted to do the NPQH (National Professional Qualification for Headship) because I wanted to speak to Headteachers on a level. I needed a school to do it at, and Pete recommended Andy who had succeeded him as Head at Campsmount when Pete retired. So that's how I found myself working with Andy when the school burnt down, and why I continued to help Andy rebuild his new school.

So, these weekly meetings were amongst all the other things we were all doing, and as they tend to do, after a while it seemed like we were talking about a dream, but not getting any closer. After about three months, Andy said to me that he thought it wouldn't be possible at Campsmount. Campsmount was a really good school, and we didn't really have the mandate to totally change it. So that's when I said. *"Ok, then we need to start a Free School."*

I remember Andy nearly falling off his chair. Time stood still. The Earth stopped revolving. The Free School policy was created by Michael Gove. It was ideologically driven by the idea that parents would demand 'grammar-like' schools, public schools you didn't have to pay for. The idea that two working class punks from Doncaster would open a Free School was the most ridiculous idea anyone had ever thought of. Ever.

After a split second (that seemed like an aeon), Andy had turned to me, looked me in the eyes and said, *"Okay, I'm in..."*. We shook hands, and the deal was done.

Andy

Like Gwyn says, this was a big deal in many different ways. I loved my role at Campsmount and I loved the area and people that we served. Like most schools in Doncaster, we served an ex-mining community which brought a fair amount of challenge but also significant reward.

We were helping and changing the mindset of our young people to believe that they could succeed and that they were capable of great things. For example, many of our students were the first people in their families to attend university, to succeed academically was to significantly change the lives of not just the young people who attended the school but also their families. And the wider community. These were the same kind of students I went to school with, they were the same as me and I was privileged to work for them. I couldn't think of another situation that would take me away from Campsmount... and then Gwyn made the call from San Diego.

I'm not as cynical as Gwyn suggests, I did go to HTH with an open mind, well, maybe half open! However, the visit to HTH put simply, changed my life. It wasn't so much the projects that students were engaged in, or the fact that the school is visually stunning in terms of curating beautiful, creative and high quality student work, but it was the way that students were able to articulate their learning in such a sophisticated and purposeful way that was the game changer for me.

I remember one student, totally unprompted, approaching us in the 'hallway' and asking if we 'wanted to see' his projects.

He proceeded to eloquently describe the narrative of his learning throughout a number of grades by taking us to artifacts, artwork and work that he had created.

The level of metacognition and depth of understanding and recall was quite frankly breathtaking. I asked myself the question 'Could my students back in Doncaster do this?' The answer was at that point a resounding and troubling, 'No.' And not because they didn't have the capability or capacity, far from it, it was because they were not being given the opportunity. On the plane home, I knew that I couldn't go back and let things stay the same.

After months of honest inaction, thinking about how we might incrementally adopt and adapt a HTH approach at Campsmount, starting in Year 7 and developing through, it became patently clear that it just wouldn't happen. The school was doing well, we'd had a good Ofsted inspection and the school was well regarded by the community. We had no imperative for change. Then Gwyn dropped the Free School bombshell. Politically, this was anathema to me and coming from a tradition of mining on my mum's side of the family and my dad being a bricklayer who did his time as an apprentice I knew there was a strong possibility no one would ever speak to me again! However, in that split second, I've never been more sure that we needed to do this, to try a different way.

So I said, 'Okay, I'm in'.

An Expedition to New England

I was rummaging around my emails, as you do, and I found my very first email from Ron Berger.

I love telling people how XP came from many critical moments – a lot of which just seem random, or serendipitous at least. I often wonder what would have happened if some of these critical things didn't happen. Or even why they actually did.

I remember reading somewhere that if you were trying to contact someone for the first time, a great tactic is to pay them a massive compliment straight away, before you ask them if they would do something for you. However, when I tell people how I got to know Ron Berger, my line is always this: I sent Ron an email out of the blue, and he nearly simply deleted it because he thought my name was spam. How different things would be if he did.

I also reflect on when Ron actually did come over to the UK, that everyone kept asking me, *"How come YOU got Ron Berger to come over to the UK???"* My answer was simple... I had asked him.

Some people would say that was 'tenacity'. I would say that I was just using my voice. Why not? If we believe we are equal, why wouldn't we use our voice?

You never know what might happen.

> As educators, we vastly underestimate the capacity of students to do great things.

Ron Berger | EL Education

Begin forwarded message:

From: Ron Berger
Subject: Re: Hello from the UK
Date: 10 July 2012 at 16:21:21 BST

Dear Gwyn,

Thank you for your kind words and your dedication to this work.

Your name (at least for me) is so unusual that I was about to delete your email as spam; at the last minute I decided to look and found that it was a real message.

I am delighted that my work and my book has been useful in the UK.

I have not been to the UK in a very long time. I get a lot of requests for presentations or consultations overseas, but my schedule is so full that I almost always turn them down. However, my wife is always asking when I will get a request from the UK, as she would love to accompany me and fit in some travel there. So I would definitely consider this.

Let me know what you are thinking.

Best wishes

Ron

Ron eventually agreed we could meet him for an hour or so on a Monday morning. This seems quite straightforward until you factor in the condition that he would meet us in Amherst, a small town in Massachusetts, USA. We had to catch a train from Doncaster to London Heathrow, then a plane to Boston USA, hire a car and drive to Amherst for an hour long meeting. So that's what we did. Luckily, we got on well, and Ron seemed impressed with our efforts and he ended up spending the whole day with us, taking us for lunch where the local restaurant offered us their speciality 'popovers' - which were actually Yorkshire puddings. Both Andy and I describe this day as the best professional development we have ever had.

We then spent a day and a half at King Middle, Portland, Maine and realised that the Expeditionary Learning (EL) model was something we could implement in the UK, blending in the best elements of HTH that we could get away with.

Mike McCarthy, the principal of King Middle said to us, *"There are two types of school; those that are improving, and those that are declining"* – I guess this would make sense when we base our school on the design process rather than a grand vision. Iterate to improve. All the time.

A pivotal moment on our trip happened at the end of the meeting with Ron, when Scott Hartl, CEO of EL leaned in and said, *"You know, it all started with you guys, right? Kurt Hahn, Gordonstoun?"* I had no idea what he was talking about. Andy explained to me on the plane home that EL came from Outward Bound, which started with a guy called Kurt Hahn. I said I knew an OB centre in Aberdovey, Wales, and it was on the plane back that we decided that it was a good idea to send all our students Outward Bound on their first day of school.

Andy

The meeting with Ron was a very humbling experience. His wisdom and insight was invaluable and his generosity overwhelming. He shared with us, out of large portfolios, the most beautiful student work I've ever seen. This wasn't unattainable stuff and the EL framework, a standards-based approach were all things we were pretty comfortable with. We were starting to see how we could amalgamate the two approaches we'd seen in the US and shape something exciting within our own context.
And it was the best CPD we'd ever had.

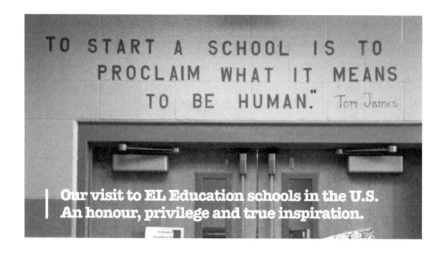

"TO START A SCHOOL IS TO PROCLAIM WHAT IT MEANS TO BE HUMAN." Tom James

Our visit to EL Education schools in the U.S. An honour, privilege and true inspiration.

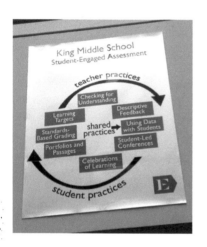

King Middle School
Student-Engaged Assessment

teacher practices

Checking for Understanding
Learning Targets
Descriptive Feedback
Standards-Based Grading
shared practices
Using Data with Students
Portfolios and Passages
Student-Led Conferences
Celebrations of Learning

student practices

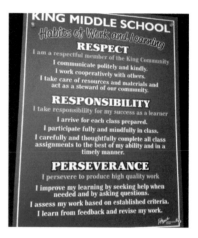

KING MIDDLE SCHOOL
Habits of Work and Learning

RESPECT
I am a respectful member of the King Community
I communicate politely and kindly.
I work cooperatively with others.
I take care of resources and materials and act as a steward of our community.

RESPONSIBILITY
I take responsibility for my success as a learner
I arrive for each class prepared.
I participate fully and mindfully in class.
I carefully and thoughtfully complete all class assignments to the best of my ability and in a timely manner.

PERSEVERANCE
I persevere to produce high quality work
I improve my learning by seeking help when needed and by asking questions.
I assess my work based on established criteria.
I learn from feedback and revise my work.

WORK HARD   GET SMART   BE NICE

Ron

I have seen many school start-ups over the past 40 years, but I have never witnessed a more remarkable beginning than that of XP. There are many reasons for this, but none more central than the heart of its founders and staff. XP is a school that embodies the message I wish all of us in education stood for: the idea that in real life we are measured not by our performance on tests, but by our character and the quality of our work. The spirit of Crew at XP is as strong as in any school I have seen. Staff and students are on a mission, together, to make the world a better place, and this is evident not just in the school's philosophy and structures, but also, importantly, in the daily examples of courage and kindness you see in hallways and classrooms.

I was fortunate to begin working with Gwyn and Andy during XP's planning phase, and as part of that process, I introduced them to EL Education schools in the U.S. On a visit to Springfield Renaissance School in Massachusetts, an urban secondary school serving low-income students (and getting 100% into college), we met with student ambassadors. The students had just begun describing the school and their lives when Gwyn apologized and ran outside. I assumed he was taking an emergency call, but when he returned he explained that he had to step outside to cry because he was so moved. And, with apologies if I embarrass Gwyn and Andy, both of them had such big hearts that this was a fairly common experience as we worked together.

How to make a school

We had to battle extremely hard to get the school building in the place we wanted and how we wanted it. When agencies present themselves as being on your side, and that we are now a team wanting to achieve the same outcome, be absolutely clear of the agenda that each organisation has, and your agenda.

While all parties wanted to build a school, the government agency wanted to build a school for the least amount of money, and the builders wanted to make a profit. These agendas are totally reasonable and understandable, but that's not how they were presented to us, so when we were being reasonable, and being totally aware that we were spending public monies, our good will was being sucked into their agendas, not our agenda of getting the best school possible.

At times, this negotiation was combative. I'm not going to pretend that it was easy. It wasn't. We had to work out what our non-negotiables were, what we were willing to sacrifice, what the greatest threat was to the project, what are the high and low risks? What is the most important thing?

At times it was very hard to stay calm, and at times, I failed.

While the Department for Education (DfE) were grateful that they didn't have to help or guide us towards opening - we knew what we were doing - we were seeing and hearing all the well-documented shenanigans that were occurring with some other Free School groups. All this hardball negotiation was done with a threat that the school might never open if we got it wrong.

It came to a crunch just before Christmas when Andy had already left his job, the Education Funding Agency were wanting us to take over a disused, run-down old Pupil Referral Unit in Balby that they could get for nothing, and we wanted a new build in central Doncaster in the newly developing Lakeside area. We came to a stand off. We said we'd walk away from the whole project if they forced the Balby site on us (this wasn't an empty threat... we would have).

Stressful times.

Andy

The reality bit when I decided to hand my resignation in to concentrate on the setting up of XP. I had XP buzzing in my brain and I knew I needed to help Gwyn without distraction; I also didn't want to let the staff and kids down at Campsmount. Even though in my heart I had made the decision, leaving a school I loved and to give up my career for a school that didn't exist except in our heads, that didn't have any staff, a building or a funding agreement was, it seemed, a massive risk. The EFA weren't being particularly helpful and I felt I needed to discuss this with my wife, Nicola. After all, we had a young daughter, Beth, who was three at the time, and a mortgage to pay.

Nicola's advice was brutally, and unsurprisingly, honest. In response to my faltering, she asked me what exactly the 'risk' was? And what would I do if XP didn't happen?

Nicola: What job do you do now?

Me: I'm a Headteacher.

Nicola: Are you any good?

Me: I'm okay, I guess.

Nicola: Then you could get another job as a Headteacher, couldn't you? And if you didn't want to do this what else could you do?

Me: Teach English?

Nicola: There you go. Then what is the risk? It will only be a risk if you don't do it.

That was the reassurance I needed.

And she was absolutely right.

As always.

It will only be a risk if you don't do it.

Doing it.

Apparently, both scenarios were presented to the Education Minister in Westminster, London, and he agreed with us. We probably got our decision because the DfE trusted us.

We were told the new school would take a year to build, so we'd need a temporary site for a year[2]. We had a great relationship with Liam Scully at Doncaster Rovers (now the CEO of Lincoln City, and still one of our Directors) and we did a deal that we would turn a 'void' under the East stand of the stadium into a corridor of four classrooms. When we left for our new build, Club Doncaster would take over the ownership for their community education.

It was a good plan. A win-win as they say.

In the meantime, we got to make our school.

Done.

Our first team.

The Boot Room.

Our first team.

2 Turned out it was a year and a term... bit uncomfortable that.

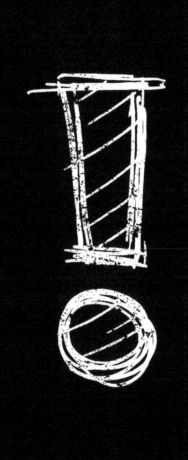

The most important thing

In my professional practice, I obsess about importance. There are so many things you can do, and they are all seen as 'important'. So how do you decide what to do next? What is the most important thing?

On my travels I have asked this question weirdly to only three people; Larry Rosenstock (High Tech High), Elliot Washor (Big Picture Learning) and Ron Berger (EL education).

So guys... out of all the important things to consider when building a school, what is the most important thing?

Larry: *"Do not segregate your kids"*

We will have mixed ability, heterogeneous classes all the way through our school.

Elliot: *"Relationships, relevance and rigour"*

So Elliot cheated and named three, but I just took the first. He said, *"schools have got it the wrong way round. It's relationships first."*

Sure enough, when Andy and I visited our first Big Picture Learning school, El Centro in North Philadelphia, USA, relationships were turned up to the max.

We will do relationships like no other school in the UK.

Ron: *"I know you're worrying about how you do projects, but that's not the most important thing. You can get projects wrong and you can fix them. But you must get your culture right."*

When we heard this, Andy and I looked at each other and breathed easy. We can do culture. Campsmount had a great culture, and it still does.

We will make a school. A school is a community. A community is a group of people that succeed *because* of their differences.

NOW!

(WELL... AGAIN...
2019...)

It was early 2019, four and a half years into the life of XP. The school was massively oversubscribed, financially secure and we'd got an outstanding Ofsted judgement the year before. Hundreds of visitors were coming to see our school from all over the world every year. We were just focusing on doing our job, but we knew that there was an appetite for other people to know what we do.

So, I was sitting with Douglas Archibald, Director of Whole Education, in the Draughtsman's Alehouse on Doncaster railway station, Platform 3, and he asked me, *"So what are the five most important things you do that other schools could take from you?"*

I said I knew the top one, but I had to think about the others...

As leaders, we have to decide on importance a lot. *"What am I going to work on right now..."* is a very complex decision, and an art we craft over the years. What is timely? What is crucial? What is easy? What can no-one else do? What is nagging me? And it all depends on context and perspective. This one was, *"what could other schools, maybe more conventional schools compared with us, get from us?"* Anyway, I thought about this over the next few days, and I came up with this list...

5 Leadership - how we operate, how we make decisions, how we decide what is important, and what isn't so much.

4 Behaviour - especially in the context we're in, we seem to be doing this well. What, why, how?

3 Curriculum - this is the most strikingly different aspect we have to other schools, so there must be a lot of takeaways there.

2 Technology - although this might be a bit boring alongside our discussion around pedagogy, we would not be the school we are, in such a short space of time, without our rabid use of collaborative technology. It's the unsung hero that all schools could do with doing.

So, for this first edition of How We XP, these will be the four 'ins' to what we do. Alongside this, we will signpost you to all the amazing work that other people have done that also explains what we do, especially EL Education. There's no need for us to redo this work just to put our own name on it. Their work is astonishing and we are proud to call them friends of XP.

The most important thing? Well, that was easy...

COMPASSION

How much do we love our children?

What does it mean to be human?

Does our school reflect the society we want to live in?

Why do we get up and go to school every morning?

What is the fire in our belly?

I want our children to explore and express who they are, respectfully, through their work.

I want our children to work with and for each other, for the greater good, beyond individual achievement.

To work hard, get smart and be kind.

To create beautiful work.

To grow.

To achieve academically.

To become the best version of themselves.

I will not treat them with impunity. I will not look down on them.

I will not subject them to punishment for non-conformity.

Because I am them, and this is what I would want for myself.

I will show them and treat them with compassion.

Above all.

Whatever it takes. I will not give up.

This is what XP looks like, feels like, sounds like.

Compassion.

Above all, compassion.

Leadership

We don't have offices.

We don't wear suits.

We share everything we do.

We actively invite critique.

We don't try to look scary.

We've got each other's backs.

We get things done.

We can make massive changes quickly.

We let the people doing it, decide how to do it.

What's good for our kids, is good for us.

We respect how hard our jobs are.

We treat each other as we would want to be treated.

We are Crew.

Now that we've got that over with, we need to share some hard facts...

We have never run a deficit, even though our schools are much smaller than a conventional secondary school.

We have never paid for cover/supply teachers.

We don't spend thousands on recruitment every year, even though as we grow, we recruit 6-10 new staff.

Our staff turnover is almost non-existent.

We have always been fully staffed.

We get the same amount of money as any other academy in the UK.

We are currently 11 (eleven) times oversubscribed for student admissions.

We have the lowest exclusion rate and highest attendance in all secondary schools in Doncaster.

We are rated as outstanding in all areas by our UK regulators, Ofsted.

The only fieldwork our students pay for is the one where we go to Spain. The school pays for Outward Bound, Duke of Edinburgh (Bronze and Silver awards), and all the fieldwork we do, which is lots eg The Globe Theatre, London. Immersion experiences such as The National Coal Mining Museum and The National Slavery Museum. Participation in launch events for our products – including art gallery and museum exhibitions, book launches at Waterstones and Jorvik Viking Festival, STEM events, Poetry Slams at Art Centres, service learning at the Yorkshire Wildlife Trust nature reserve, local museums, theatres, shopping centres - the latter for Expedition research, engagement and beautiful work displays we deliver. We also support and take students to visit our local food bank and centres run by AGE UK.

In other words, our school is run extremely efficiently, our staff and students work extremely hard, we get immersed in loads of experiences, and generally speaking, we are very happy. Students, staff and parents.

This doesn't mean we're perfect. We are far from it. We make mistakes, and we want to improve almost all aspects of our school, as we know we can do it better.

But our approach is working.

We know a lot of schools have issues with recruitment, money and behaviour. While our kids still make mistakes and drive us crazy, we don't have the same level of issues on any of these three big things.

We think this is down to our whole school approach, and to make what we do accessible, we've broken this analysis down into the four chapters on leadership, behaviour, curriculum and technology.

This chapter is about leadership, and the best way we've found to explain what we do, is to break down our approach into little chunks[3]. Anecdotes linked to solid example. Driving these anecdotes is single minded purpose. Everything we do must have a purpose. We must be clear about this, or we won't do it.

We are no way near the finished article, and we never will be, so the concept of importance also drives our decision making. What will we do next?

We have tried to group these chunks to create some semblance of cohesion, but it's not a jigsaw puzzle, it's complex links. These chunks are glimpses, windows and perspectives into the whole messy, complicated network of a bunch of people working together.

We hope some of these things will chime with you, make you curious, make you think about your practice, make you want to push back at us, but ultimately allow you to reflect and make our children, colleagues, schools and society better people and places to live with and in.

You can do this.

---

3 A big appreciation to Jason Fried & David Heinemeier Hansson (Basecamp, Rework), and James Watt (Brewdog, Business for Punks) for showing me the way. Your work is reflected in mine.

Why we are here, and what we are playing with

Most schools have a sense of why they exist.

I'll be honest and say, in most schools I've visited in the UK, this sense of purpose tends to be created by the headteacher. It is a 'vision' and often comes and goes with the headteacher.

The most successful schools I have seen have a clear sense of purpose that exists within most of the staff. Whether it is a KIP school (Knowledge Is Power) or an EL school (Expeditionary Learning), this sense of why we are here is strong. Staff and students can articulate this purpose clearly and simply and can then build on this in terms of, what does this look like in reality. The why, how and what.

In a perfect world, we would pursue our core purpose relentlessly, with an infinite supply of resources that we would lavish on our children, and in ten years, humanity will have populated the stars.

But the world isn't perfect. Perfection doesn't exist. We have to live in reality, and we can choose to either fight this fact, or work with it.

In a perfect world, the purpose of our school might look like this:

1 Our students become beautiful people

2 Our students create beautiful work...

3 ...and make the world a better place

4 All our students can access their next destination

5 Happy parents

In reality, the reasons our school even exists are in this ordered list:

1 Financial stability

2 Good academic outcomes

3 Outstanding Ofsted rating

4

5 Full admissions

6 Fully staffed

7

8 High attendance

9 Low exclusions

10

11 Happy parents

To qualify this list, I have missed a few numbers out to signify the big jump between each set of outcomes, for instance, high attendance is not just below being fully staffed, it's way below. Also, to exist I know we only need a 'Good' Ofsted rating, but for us to do what we want to do, we need it to be outstanding.

Years ago, I used to have many arguments about this. Well, I say arguments, but maybe it was more of a whinge-fest – everyone agreed. What a terrible state of affairs. Now, when people mention this terrible state of affairs, I just agree quietly and say, 'yeah', and then get on with my job.

XP exists because the government gives us money to provide an education for our children for free. Now that's pretty cool, and whatever we believe should be happening, this didn't used to happen and often doesn't happen in other countries. This money may not be enough to do everything, but in my experience, it's enough to do lots of great things, and again, that's cool with me.

And while this money has strings attached, our government do give us a tremendous amount of freedom, lots of which the schools in our country don't take advantage of. Yes, some of these freedoms are more perception than reality, but hey, we are the proof of these freedoms because we do what we do!

Finally, if you look at the top three, there is only really the 'good academic outcomes' point that cripples us. Not because we don't want our students to get smarter - absolutely, we do - but the way this is measured is the most unbelievably bonkers thing that we as adults inflict on our children in the modern world. But hey, ho...

So, while we try our best to achieve the top list, we are acutely aware of the second. We are extremely proud that we achieve all of them, and we only have one beef about how point 2 is measured. And while that beef is more like the size of a galactic frozen McDonalds warehouse, we are achieving our perfect world purpose and the reality of us even existing at all.

We can do this because we know what we're playing with.

We talk about the kind of work we do (good or bad). We talk about the perceived rules we play to (reality or shared myth?). We look at evidence and research and its actual validity. We discuss opposites, i.e. If we don't do X, Y will happen. And we get real with 'data' and most of all, money.

We work hard at this. We are tough with each other. We push each other's ideas and conceptions. We are not guessing. We aren't experimenting. We don't have a 'faith' in a certain ideology. And we don't just do things because everyone else does.

If we did, we'd have bought the birdy song.

Good work, bad work and eating frogs

Good work is the work we love doing. It excites us and we talk about it to others, and we wake up on a Saturday morning and want to finish it off. We seem to have an infinite amount of energy available to us to do our good work.

Bad work is the work we hate doing. It stresses us out and we don't see the point, but we eventually make ourselves do it, or we try to leave it and worry about being found out. It takes us ten times as long to do bad work than good work.

At XP, we try to do as much good work as possible, and hardly any bad work. That's why our teachers work really hard, generally talk about work at work (and at home...), and we can boast numbers like 99%+ teacher attendance and £0 spent on cover teachers.

> I've never worked so hard, and enjoyed my work, as much as I have at XP.

Kerry Poncia | Teacher | XP East

The trick is, we always start with the purpose. Why are we doing this? Most of the work we do makes sense.

Sometimes, bad work can be converted into good work by explaining the purpose. If the purpose is that it will effectively benefit the kids, that's normally enough. Sometimes staff need reminding of the purpose. I have genuinely seen frowns turn into smiles and skips through a short chat about why we do things.

Sometimes bad work is bad because there's a perceived barrier to getting it done. Again, removing that barrier (ie offering support, giving access to resources) often results in energised staff.

Sometimes, when bad work is just bad, and it has no purpose, but you have to do it, you can manage it through justification. For instance, we talk about our Ofsted judgement as being our 'economic driver'.

We don't really see the purpose, but we need an 'outstanding' judgement to do what we want to do. I guess, we make up a purpose, and it makes us a little bit happier to do it.

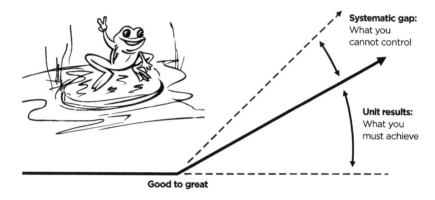

Systematic gap: What you cannot control

Unit results: What you must achieve

Good to great

This graph from Jim Collin's, 'Good to Great and the social sectors' shows us that because we have the privilege of receiving money from the government for doing what we do, there are things we can't control. This puts a positive spin on 'bad work' and it allows us to identify and understand them, and why we ultimately need to do it. This allows us to not say, *"Ofsted are a pain"* and allows us to say, *"Ofsted are our economic driver. We need an outstanding Ofsted judgement to do what we need to do."*

It helps turn bad work into good work. If bad work is just bad - there's no purpose, and we don't have to do it, not really... then don't do it.

Do what is right, not what is expected.

If we can't do any of this, we just eat the frog[4].

Don't procrastinate. Just identify the frog and get it done. First thing in the morning. It will be the worst thing you'll do all day, and once you've done it, you'll be proud that you have.

If you need to sack someone, prepare for it, then get it done. First thing in the morning... and if you have two frogs to eat, eat the worst one first.

---

4 From the phrase, *'If you eat a frog in the morning, you'll do nothing worse for the rest of the day'.* The etymology of this phrase proves that we are nothing but stories... https://quoteinvestigator.com/2013/04/03/eat-frog/

Shared myths

A shared myth is something almost everyone believes in. Some are really useful, and some are really bad and need destroying. The trick is to spot them, understand them, and make them up if it benefits you.

A good shared myth to start with is money. Money in itself isn't worth anything. We all believe it is, so we exchange things that are worth something (food, clothes, beer, music etc) for this mythical thing called 'money'.

Money used to be gold coins, which was (and still is) believed to be 'worth' something, because it's rare, or some tenuous excuse like that.

Nowadays, money has been reduced first to worthless metal, then paper, then plastic and now it exists purely as numbers.

Depending on how much we believe in it, depends on how much we believe it is worth. This results in the worth of different monies fluctuating up and down. Bitcoin is a great example to show this. Economic crashes also shows this well.

But generally, money allows us to simplify the transaction of goods, which is good, but it also distorts the wealth of individuals, creates wars and the class system which is bad (depending on whether you are rich or not).

But it's definitely a shared myth.

Law, government and fashion are others. God, Queen and Country. These things exist because we believe in them.

In schools, there are many things that are generally accepted as true, but are actually nonsense.

They are made up.

Here are some examples:

The more you pay, the better the person you get.

Small schools are financially unviable.

Mixed ability classes hold back the most able.

If you don't have a school uniform, you get bullying and you can tell who the poor kids are.

MATs can't work over large distances.

Progressive teaching techniques create behavioural issues with working class kids.

Employers care about the GCSEs you got.

Teaching by talking at people is the traditional way of learning.

We must subject children to intense sets of final exams to know what they are good at. (Or a recent spin on this is, to know how good the school is)

Parents demand 'tough, zero-tolerance' behaviour policies and strict uniforms.

I could go on for ages about these myths, but I can't be bothered. They just aren't true. Great schools are great schools.

You can defeat shared myths by not believing anything until you see it, and feel it. And then it has to be a good person/school failing at it, not a bad one. Bad schools are bad schools.

Lies

In education, lies are normally called 'research' - or worse still, 'evidence'.

In education, research is something that is done on a system that is impossible to have a 'control' eg a school.

Imagine the most complex car engine you can. Now imagine having two, side by side. Change a component in one and compare the output of both. Speed, fuel efficiency, oil burnt, air needed, pollution produced, reliability. Now change the type of oil in one and test them again. Now the temperature of the environment.

Now change every component in this complex engine and replace it with a person.

And do the same with the other engine.

Only you can't use the same people... obviously.

Now, put your foot on the accelerator person and measure the exhaust person's output. Do the same with the other engine, and see if you get the same result.

Yeah.

Research in schools is a problem.

The only output that most people trust are the academic outcomes of standards-based tests. To the extent that other measurable outputs like attendance and exclusions don't seem to be as important so much.

I don't think I've ever seen data comparing schools on how much students have grown as characters or the beauty in their work.

In the UK we are spending millions of pounds on research.

We seem to be doing this to produce headlines, not truth.

Well, that's what's happening anyway.

The best research I've seen is based on deep case studies, of similarities between different schools. Of why certain schools are different, and what this produces. Stories that inspire and that are true. Stories about exceptional practice.

Most research based on numbers tend to look at lots of schools and report on the average results of a certain intervention.

This assumes that all schools are the same, or they ignore the 'outliers' which smooths out their results. That is, schools that have achieved exceptional outcomes, and schools that have achieved terrible outcomes, get wiped from the results to produce an average.

The logic behind this is, if your school implements this intervention, what is the likely outcome?

We should not be interested in the average.

We should be interested in the exceptional, and why those schools that create exceptional outcomes, whatever those outcomes are, can do just that.

I look out for research that has deep case studies, looking at outcomes wider than just academic ones (but also including these), and where schools have done something exceptional.

I then visit these schools, because I need to know that it is true.

As school leaders, we must be in each other's schools all the time, sharing best practice, stealing from each other. Pushing, questioning each other. This is the best research we can do.

Opposites

I read in a comic a concept about 'opposites'. The line was, *'The opposite of war isn't peace; it's making love'* (although they didn't quite use those exact words...)

Like the opposite of love isn't hate. It's indifference.

So what are we playing with regarding opposites?

When you look at arguments in education, some people make their arguments based on false opposites... if we don't do this, then we will get that. Some call them false dichotomies. I view these things as two sides of a coin, and sometimes, the only difference between the two sides is perception.

The opposite of sadness isn't happiness; it's ambition.

Maybe this coin has written on one side, 'ignorance is bliss', and on the other, 'anger is an energy'.

The universe is unthinkably massive, therefore:

1   We are insignificant so there's no point in life
2   This gives us total freedom to do what we want.

I guess this is a little more sophisticated than the glass is half full/empty concept. I have found it to be incredibly powerful, especially in schools.

Take rigour for instance. One way to ensure the 'how do I know' part of rigour, is to have a sophisticated hierarchical leadership process in place that systematically and regularly checks that what you want to happen is happening.

Another way is to make what we do, public. The former is high energy hierarchical scrutiny, the latter is low energy, distributed and celebratory.

So when we want to ensure rigour, we ask ourselves, *"how can we make this work public?"*

The opposite of hierarchical scrutiny isn't negligence; it's public celebration.

Garbage In, Garbage Out

The term GIGO (Garbage In, Garbage Out) is an acronym from computing that flashes in big neon letters in front of my eyes every time I look at 'data'.

Data in schools has been turned into an industry, much like the cosmetic and fashion industry, based on lies. False desires to make the analysis of schools and children simple, by turning complex behaviours into numbers that we can then compute.

Paraphrasing Einstein, *"Make everything as simple as possible, but no simpler..."*, this has turned dangerous.

Every school is judged by one word. Outstanding, Good, Requires Improvement[5] and Inadequate.

Every kid is reduced to a set of numbers.

Worse, this garbage is then applied to 'groups' of students, that are somehow connected because they share the same sex, demographic, a 'Special Educational Need' and then interventions are put in place to ensure these groups 'catch up'.

Now, I'm not saying that kids with SEN don't need extra support, but clumping them all together to try and get some meaningful analysis of this 'group', when SEN can range from anything to everything, is meaningless.

You get this research published, and the headline is written whether the data is secure, or not.

I find it all absolutely bonkers. Extremely costly and extremely ineffective in helping our children become the best version of themselves.

Using this garbage out, we can cherry pick our headlines and drive our ideology. Suffice to say, standards-based testing gives numbers that are easy to manipulate in spreadsheets, so any education that produces children that perform well in these tests are seen as being successful over things that can't be measured as well, or as accepted.

---

5 I know... I know...! I can count... jeez...

Ultimately, by worshiping this garbage, we end up with stressed kids and teachers, rising mental health issues, high exclusions of low ability, low income children with SEN, low attendance and kids who are not prepared for the real world where success is NOT achieved by standards-based tests.

The final ridicule is that GCSE results don't particularly matter that much. They open doors, but it is who you are, and the quality of the work you produce that get you the job, the place at university, the start-up business loan.

For schools in the UK, in 2019 at least, they are the be all and end all, and in the end, it is our children that suffer.

XP's compromise is that we prepare our students for these tests so we can exist. We try to ensure that students' success in exams are a consequence of our curriculum, focusing on creating beautiful work and character growth.

It's tough.

Back to data - my only question is, *"Is this useful information?"* - Do the numbers tell us something we can act on that will improve our school and impact meaningfully on our children?

If not, it's garbage.

Money, Money, Money

As leaders, we are ultimately responsible for how we use the resources we have available to us. Whether it be buildings, kit, books, staff, time or anything else, this ultimately boils down to MONEY.

Don't be shy.

In fact, you CANNOT be shy.

As Friedrich Nietzsche, the famous accountant once said, *"Gaze long into the spreadsheet, and the numbers will gaze into thee"*.

You HAVE TO know every single line on your budget.

We call it 'staring into the brutal reality of truth'.

Open that old drawer, and get everything out. Lift that stone and see the mud and creepy crawlies. Stamp on them, or nurture them, but you must KNOW them.

The issues I see in schools today is that most Head Teachers/Principals/ CEOs were teachers promoted into these positions, and many have not felt the burn of running a commercial business of needing that sale to pay the staff member who needs that money to put food on the plates of their children. That is hard, sometimes desperate and very important work.

While the powers that be mess around with school funding, it is by and large much more predictable than a commercial business, and I guess it allows leaders to let things tick over 'as they always have done'. This is comfortable.

When it comes to numbers, I am a complete fascist about the simple formula that INCOME - EXPENDITURE = WHAT YOU HAVE LEFT. I need to know what it is, why we need it, how we could reduce it if it's a cost or increase it if it's an income. It is not a 'cheap is best' approach, it is very much a 'what is best value'.

With technology, we buy both Chromebooks and Apple to illustrate this point. Both provide excellent value for money, where PCs don't in my opinion. PCs swim in that comfortable sea of 'everyone else uses them, so...'

We don't mess about.

Energy consumption needs to be as close to zero as it can be without us being cold.

I remember a conversation with our cleaning company when I said, *"The school is amazingly clean, like it sparkles"*. They mistook this statement for a compliment, when in fact it was a problem to me as I knew we must be spending too much on cleaning. Schools don't need to sparkle, they need to be cleanish/not noticeably dirty. Good enough is good enough.

Before you recruit someone else to give you more capacity, you have to feel the hurt, or you end up with loads of staff doing stuff with no purpose.

The opposite of being comfortable is being effective.

What would you do if your business manager disappeared? If this strikes fear into your heart, you need to stare, stare and stare some more.

The reason you need to do this is because you will find that you have more money than you thought, and you can then spend this wisely and improve the experience of your students and staff.

Please remember, more money doesn't necessarily mean better. I recently had a quote for our new school to be kitted out with AV equipment for £180,000. Instead, I worked with an AV expert who I trusted, and we implemented a better system for £40,000.

Better means simpler, easier, faster, more reliable.

CEOs paid more than the Prime Minister of the country is the opposite of this. Offer more money, and you will often just end up with someone who desires more money. No matter how you try to justify it, I can think of much better ways to spend £150,000 than on just one person. Don't tell me that no-one else could do it, it is simply not true.

Leading an organisation starts and ends with money. Organisations wouldn't exist otherwise.

You can't eat dreams or good intentions and money is only real when it's in your proverbial pocket.

Making good decisions

So, we know what we're playing with. We know why we are here, our purpose. Now, what do we want to create? This is where design principles come in.

I try to explain design principles like this:

Instead of a school, think about a kettle. A simple kitchen appliance. Let's say you have had many kettles in your time and you are frustrated by them. They break, they leak, they don't look great, they're not efficient etc.

You think you have a new idea for a kettle. You go to a designer and you say, *"I want you to help me build a new kettle"*.

A good designer would say, *"No you don't. What do you actually want to do? What problem do you want to solve?"*

Maybe you come up with something like, *"I want to be able to safely, quickly and cheaply deliver boiling water into a cup or pan."*

Maybe you don't create a kettle. But you solve the problem.

Design principles are a distillation of the problem you want to solve. They are not the solution. They are the big picture that guides you to make the right decisions, that you keep revisiting to see if you're on the right track. They don't tell you what to do. They tell you what not to do.

We adopted and adapted High Tech High's design principles into this:

Personalisation

• we express who we are through our work
• we forge our own pathways to career, university and life readiness
• we have ownership of our own progress and learning

Connect with the world

• we learn naturally across subjects from enquiry through to presentation to authentic audiences
• we create meaningful relationships beyond the classroom
• we engage in relevant work that matters

A common mission

- we form genuine communities with shared goals
- we have collaborative accountability
- we take real risks to achieve more
- we are 'Crew' not passengers

Teachers are learners

- we learn through the design process
- we have ownership of the curriculum
- we are accountable to our stakeholders

Language is our culture

- we actively refer to our character values each day, using them as a framework for our conduct, they are not just words on walls
- we realise our values through our Habits of Work and Learning
- we use sign language and common phrases when appropriate to express our thoughts, feelings and sense of community

If you visit our school, you will see these design principles manifest throughout our school. If we do something that doesn't fit with these principles, we stop doing it.

We have refined them over the years, and so have HTH. On their website at **www.hightechhigh.org/about-us** you will see they have simplified and clarified theirs to Equity, Personalization[6], Authentic Work and Collaborative Design. You can see how Equity was 'A Common Intellectual Mission'. Authentic Work was 'Connect with the Adult World' and Collaborative Design was 'Teachers as Designers'. Hopefully you can see the alignment and slight differences we made.

We know that instead of 'Teachers are learners', it should be 'We are all learners', but we wanted to get this message out to our teachers, as this is the most important problem to solve. Teachers often, and understandably I guess, see themselves as the expert. It's easy and forgivable to do if you are standing in front of thirty kids all day, every day, and extolling your knowledge on them.

---

6 Spelt wrong for some reason... (American joke!)

The point we are making and the problem we need to solve is that teachers need to learn their craft and get better every day. We need to be pedagogical geeks, or 'pedageeks'. Remind me to register that URL.

To have this big picture, defined by our design principles is extremely powerful when we determine the purpose of all the different things we do. Why do we do it? Why is it important?

Design principles can overlap, but they cannot be mutually exclusive, obviously.

Our design principles fit well with EL's Core Practices as well. I remember when Ron showed me this document years ago, I said is was like 'future me' handing over my life's work to me now. It's an amazing document and a bible for schools. When you have over 160 schools, as EL does, and so many great people working in them, this is what you can achieve.

HTH's genius is in its implicit simple purity. EL's genius is its explicit model of practice.

Building, rebuilding, rebooting and tuning

We built XP from a blank sheet of paper. We recognise this is an experience that not many people working in education have. We often get people saying, *"I wish I could build my school from scratch, it's so much easier than to change what you've inherited".*

For those people who say this, I say, *"well you obviously haven't started a school from scratch then, coz it's tremendously hard!!!"*

But, I know what they mean. Still, I can't wait for XP to be full so I have the model in front of me to tweak and tune. To rebuild, reboot and transition.

The school will never be 'finished'. We will always be evolving.

And because a school is a group of people, we need to reboot. This is about fighting entropy. When we started, we were often asked, *"where do you get the teachers to do these amazing Expeditions?"* and we say, they are just good people who we work with to become good Expeditionary teachers. We were then asked, *"but don't they just default back to being a normal teacher?"*

I hated this idea.

That there was some kind of natural 'default' that we fall back into, and that looks like what some would describe as 'traditional teaching' – standing in front of kids, talking at them.

No, the traditional teacher is not a natural default. What is natural is the human nature to take the 'easiest option', and the easiest option for a teacher is to rock up every morning, stand in front of the kids, 'teach' them, then go home and get paid.

This is not a default, this is entropy, and to fight entropy you need to inject energy, and in this case, the energy is the right information at the point of need.

When our teachers don't do what they are supposed to do, it's not because they are bad people, it's because they focus on what they deem to be urgent, rather than what is actually important. It is up to leaders to ensure that our teachers understand what is important, and get those important things done.

Teaching is intense, and it is so easy to focus on planning the next lesson rather than stepping back and looking at the big picture, the Expedition overview, looking at risks and mitigating those risks.

If we are not supporting and challenging our teachers to do the right things, we lose our battle with entropy, and we get teachers just teaching stuff[7] to kids. We can do better than this.

Sometimes, this requires a 'reboot'. This is when we go back to basics and we remind ourselves the purpose of immersion, of fieldwork, of authentic products, etc.

Every year, the first week, we reboot Crew. Because if we get Crew right, we get everything right.

---

7 The old teacher joke about teaching your dog to sing fits nicely here... *"I taught my dog to sing yesterday"*, *"What? Your dog can sing?"*, *"Of course not! I said I 'taught' my dog to sing..."* - telling them, and them being able to do it are two different things.

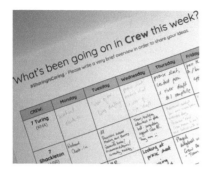

Sometimes things just need a little tuning. Ron told me that when he visits schools, he observes their tuning. What are they tight on, and what's not so much, what's loose? This can sometimes just be little reminders in staff Crew, then a follow up at the point of need - a whisper in the ear, when it is happening.

Sometimes things need rebuilding. We look at where we are, what we do, and we make big changes quickly. This is normally with a staff working group, so we get staff voice and buy in. We invite everyone, and those that can be bothered to turn up, get heard. Then these staff implement it.

Back to tuning. I have this theory I'm working on. It's called the **'200% theory'**. It goes like this. If you just leave stuff up to good people, and you don't fight the entropy, they'll get maybe 80% right. If you're fighting the entropy, you can get it up to 95%. But in the cases where you want to be really tight, and you spend that extra energy on the last 5% and get things perfect, you seem to enter into some kind of magical nirvana. It's like it doubles. That last 5% then becomes 200% – that's the perception. We see that happen every now and again when we get things right. Most of the time it happens in exhibitions, when the students just somehow step up and do things you have never seen before. That's what makes adults cry.

Know the job

There are many ways to lead. The way I choose to build our school is by doing a job first, then getting someone better than me to do that job.

One job Andy and I can't let go is teaching. While I'm not the best teacher in the world, I need to feel the pressure of our core business. Andy teaches far too much and I hope he's reading this.

I don't feel I can ask someone to do something well, unless I have at least done it once, badly.

We call this practice, 'digging the seams' - our leaders can work directly with children, while changing the school policy, and working with everyone in between. I did this recently with SEN (Special Educational Needs) interventions. I chose a student that we were most struggling with as a 'case study'. I discovered that our teachers and learning coaches knew lots about the behaviours of the student, but were unclear about what strategies to use that work best to support and challenge them. I discovered that we had written pages and pages of information about the student (like two documents totalling about 24 pages long), but the information in there 1. Didn't have clarity, and 2. Wasn't shared with the staff interacting with the student. Good work, but a total waste of time and energy! I discovered the processes of how we form strategies and ensure staff know what to do, and are actually doing it, were not effective. So as a leader, I went from child through to policy to change and improve all this.

There is absolutely no point in a hierarchical system where leaders change only policy when it has minimal impact on the child.

When you can share this improvement process and include staff in the improvements, through collaborative technologies (like Google Docs), that becomes extremely powerful.

When I've done a job, and I want to delegate it, I try to make clear that I'm delegating the outcomes, not the activity. I say, this is how I've done it, but it's the outcomes that matter.

I try to delegate the doing AND the thinking.

Three very big things

1 The biggest single factor in a classroom on progress of learning is the quality of the teacher.

2 The biggest indicator of outcomes for a student is their home environment.

3 The biggest factor of how good a school is, is the quality of its leadership.

HOME . CLASSROOM . SCHOOL

To create a great school, we should focus on improving the quality of teaching, the connection between home and school, and leadership capacity and capability.

Home

We know our students well, and that means their parents/carers and their home life as well.

We maximise positive relationships through parental leadership in school and expertise/other contributions.

We minimise negative relationships by breaking down perceived barriers, regular positive communication (no alarms and no surprises), and creating a safe haven at school for students.

Classroom

We create and deliver the curriculum together and hold each other to account, supporting and challenging each other daily. This is constant professional development. We are open, honest and transparent.

Only when someone does something on their own and doesn't share it publicly, should we be worried that they might not be developing or producing work of quality – so don't do this.

School

Everyone knows how our school works. Governors, staff, students and parents. This is distributed leadership.

Good enough is good enough

Don't let the pursuit of perfection get in the way of a good enough solution. Perfection is the enemy of 'done'. Good enough is good enough.

Time and energy has never been wasted so much on the pursuit of perfection. I have seen so many meetings get consumed by unimportant details.

Get the most important things sorted first. Once this is done, then you can sweat the small stuff. You can deal with grey areas if you have covered off 90% of the problem.

In the 70s, there was a vision of supersonic flight. Concorde was created and it was beautiful. Yet Concorde is now a thing of the past and we fly around in Boeings. I'm not saying that's amazing, I'd love to travel to New York on Concorde, but it had a total passenger capacity of 100 and consumed the same amount of fuel as a Boeing 747, while the 747 could fly twice as far and had four times the passenger capacity. This means I can fly to New York and back for £250. That's amazing.

It's the same in the design world. Most designers create amazing chairs. The Charles Eames lounge chair is a classic and very desirable. But the plastic moulded chair won. Why? Because they are cheap, do the job and are stackable.

There is a difference between getting it right and getting it perfect. Beauty cannot exist without imperfection.

It is about what is most important, not what is perfect.

Brick walls

Sometimes we come up against an issue that we know isn't right and we need to make it better. Some things are easy to change and others feel like massive brick walls in our way, and they can seem insurmountable, so we don't do the right thing and we accept the status quo.

We can't be blamed. There's a brick wall in front of us, right?

Well, that depends. How important is it to do the right thing? Is there a way round it? Is there a way under it? Is there a way over it?

Or is there a way through it?

At the times when you must do the right thing, I reflect on Isaac Newton's second law of motion. What happens when the unstoppable force meets the immovable block?

The trick is to believe in doing the right thing. If you are certain you are doing the right thing, you do not care what happens.

Become the unstoppable force and brace for impact!

But this isn't just about smashing things up. There are other times when you yourself cannot move. Your 'red lines'. You put everything on the line for these moments and you become the immovable object.

Brace for impact!!

Whatever happens, do the right thing, not what is expected of you. A decision based on values is not wrong. You may be able to make better decisions, but you are not wrong.

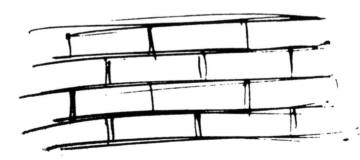

Time and money

I have never said to anyone, *"No you can't. There's no money"*, because there is always money.

Money is just like time. We choose how we spend it.

You can make money (spend less, sell more) and you can make time (hire or re-prioritise staff).

So we ask our staff to win the argument. Why do we need more staff? Why do we need more science resources? Why do we need to go to Auschwitz?

The best way for staff to make the right decision is to make it real and put them in charge of a pot of money. Let them do the balancing act because they will often come up with an impactful alternative.

We often ask staff to model ideas with what we've got already.

Ask them, *"so what would that look like?"* - ideas can often be discounted if you can't draw it / map it / get close to it with existing technology.

When you do have a model, you can clearly see what needs to happen to make it real.

You can see the real purpose instead of an idea that might sound cool but isn't.

Necessity is the mother of invention – not scarcity.

The having of wonderful ideas, and some good ones

I once thought it would be a good idea to have a school motto – and translate it to Latin. How bad is that idea? So I thought it could be in Welsh instead, but it doesn't take away from the fact that it was a really bad idea in the first place.

The best way to have good ideas is to have lots of ideas.

Linus Pauling | Multiple Nobel Prize winner

Anyway, I thought a good motto would be, 'From the shoulders of giants, to the stars' as a metaphor for the journey of our school from the origins of EL and HTH to the ultimate aim for humanity.

"Gigantium humeris insidentes, ad astra"

Told you it was a bad idea!.

The worst idea ever is that it's good to be the 'ideas guy' - no, it's not! If you're the person that likes to have ideas in meetings and then expect others to make your ideas happen, STOP IT.

My To Do list isn't called 'To Do', I call it my 'Ideas' list. They are only ideas until they get done.

Ideas need to go through the 'bad idea filter' of a few people, with the 'good enough' setting set to ON. The default answer is no. The questions to then ask, are:

• What does that look like?
• How can we model that with what we've got?
• What are the risks and how can we mitigate them?
• What is the impact on the child compared with the energy we need to put into it?

There are lots of ways to make decisions.

Our design principles don't tell us what to do, they tell us what not to do. If we have an idea and it clashes with our design principles, we don't do it.

There are lots of choices that don't really matter. Uniform or no uniform. Vertical or horizontal Crews. We know this because there are successful schools that have implemented either.

The decision isn't important. It's understanding the purpose of the decision that makes it right for you.

Often you get different opinions on how to do something and sometimes you can't get a consensus. When this happens, remember the following:

- Everybody's got an opinion. This isn't devaluing voice, it's saying that there are many ways to do things, so share the air, step up and step back.
- Don't let someone who doesn't have the responsibility of delivering, dictate how something gets done.
- Give someone a chance.
- Pocket a decision – say, ok... you do it your way this time, but next time I decide.
- Beware of false dichotomies - embrace the genius of the 'and', not the tyranny of the 'or'.
- Don't make bad decisions for other people – often I've heard stuff like, *'oh the LA won't like that, and even though I disagree with them, we best not do it.'* - Forget that - If we want to do something, let them stop us.
- If someone is leading, let them make the decision - just don't let anything go against your design principles.
- An imperfect solution is not a reason to not do it, if it's good enough.

Sometimes the right decision is not to do anything at all - or just keep doing what you are already doing.

Rules that don't exist

The summer holidays in England are six weeks long. I think in America they are even longer.

I think we have summer holidays because we used to work in the fields. I think it's an old agricultural thing. I got told that was the reason in America anyway.

Everyone knows that they are too long. They drag and kids forget everything and get into bad habits.

Four weeks is enough to have a really good break and a rest. So we started with a four week holiday.

However, when stuff happens that you've got to deal with, four weeks is really tight. So now we have a five week holiday.

We also have fifteen 'staff days'. These are days we use where kids aren't in the school and we do planning and tackle any issues or implement whole school changes.

Every other school in England that I know has five staff days. So we have three times as many. We started with ten but we thought we needed some more.

School opens from 8 to 4:30 for kids. Sessions are from 8:30 to 3:15 – not sure why, it's just what we do. Some schools in England do longer school days because they believe they get better results. Yey them.

I was hosting a school on their visit to XP and they asked me how did we get to have 15 staff days. I answered, *"coz you can"*. I asked them if they were an academy and they said yes, and I told them that they could do that too. You just decide to do it. They didn't believe me so I showed them the line in our funding agreement that says academies set the school times and calendar.

I then said if you could make a school that only had the kids for a week but could show academic progress, then that would be ok too.

Schools have never had as much freedom. Don't enforce rules that don't exist. Do what makes sense.

Start as you mean to go on

On the first day of school, all our children go Outward Bound. Our staff have a similar outdoor experience from their first day too. What's good enough for our kids is good enough for us.

Throughout this experience, we explore the meaning of 'Crew', our character traits, habits of work and learning, what it means to have a common mission, and experience various protocols such as circling up, degunge and leave no trace.

These are all done in conditions that are unfamiliar and generally outside most of our comfort zones.

We then bring all of this back into school - into our classrooms.

And we never stop referring back to this starting position.

From a staff perspective, we know everyone has gone through this. Even our administration staff. When things get tough, we remind ourselves that every single person in our organisation is a decent human being, and we are all Crew.

This is a great leveller, and a great platform to support and challenge each other. This allows us to keep our expectations of each other extremely high and allows us to be open, honest and transparent about our practices.

The first day is the foundation of our culture.

The jigsaw puzzle

I used to, and many other people still see schools as a jigsaw puzzle. The idea that a school can be split up into neat little pieces, like Curriculum, Assessment, Pastoral etc and then, building on this, that different systems can be dropped in, or swapped out.

This creates the idea that you can look at a process as an 'intervention', and trial it at different schools and measure its impact. This is often called 'research'.

This assumes that all schools are generally 'the same', and the average must be the probable impact if you implement it at your school.

Schools are much more complex than this!

Make things as simple as possible, but no simpler.

Albert Einstein (paraphrase)

When we talk about our schools, and how we might be able to improve them, we always have to consider the whole. Schools are more like interlinked neural networks than jigsaws, with each neuron being a person. That person can change, so you can't have a neat picture on the box to slot shapes into. Changing one person can change the whole picture.

We often create 'theoretical models' of staff structures, then create a good enough real one!

When we consider the effectiveness of a process, we always consider the people carrying them out.

To look at the whole effect of a change, we refer to this as looking at the system through a coloured filter, where each different colour is the 'piece', eg red is curriculum, blue is pastoral etc, so we see the red or blue highlight across the whole system. It is a metaphor for recognising the complexity of the behaviours within school, and to recognise this is best complemented with simple rules.

Simple rules begat complex behaviours[8]

This is our dress code: 'Please dress appropriately and modestly.'

The result of this is that we don't spend very much time at all discussing the clothes our students wear. Our students think about what is appropriate and what 'modest' means. Our students wear many different items of clothing and the vast majority are appropriate and modest.

About once a year, some students appeal to me to look at pushing the boundaries, I push back and ask them to have the conversation with their Crew leader, which they normally don't, and that's that for the year.

Compare this with most other schools with school uniforms. Think about how much resource is spent policing the uniform policy. Every day.

And for what end?

Complicated rules begat simple behaviours, and the more complicated a system is, the more likely it is to fail.

Please remember... 'Complex is not the same as complicated.'

We want complex behaviours!

This is what humans are good at, and how we beat the robots.

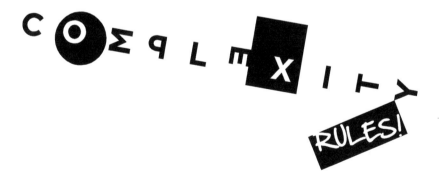

---

8 Thanks to Larry Rosenstock - I got this from him. No idea where he got it from...

Risks and how to mitigate them

We've established our purpose, what we're playing with and how we try and make the best decisions. But nothing goes right all the time.

In ensuring we're doing our best, we have to look at things in terms not just of importance, but in terms of risk and how we can mitigate them.

Risks are often things that we do naturally as people, and if we identify them and work out the opposite, this mitigates their risk to our organisation.

What are the traps that we can fall into?

How does XP stay XP despite all these distractions?

Everyone knows how we work

The first thing every visitor to XP experiences is an ambassador tour. This is led by two or more peer-selected ambassador students (around half our students are ambassadors[9], but any student could run a tour) who guide visitors around our school, explaining what we do and why we do it.

Our students eloquently describe the constituent parts of Expeditions, classroom protocols, assessment processes, restorative behaviour practices and answer any questions our visitors have as they guide them through the school, going into sessions and talking through our curated Expeditions on the walls of our schools.

We do not train our students how to do this because we have not had to - they learn from each other.

Our Trust directors are a majority of parents, as are our school governors.

We often form 'working groups' to work through issues such as communication, stewardship etc which will involve people from all our stakeholder groups that want a say.

Teachers, learning coaches, administration, students, parents, governors – we all know how our school works.

This is what we call distributed leadership.

We have all seen what happens to schools who depend on one person to lead - the cult of the headteacher - it won't and cannot happen at XP.

---

9 Actually, we used to do this, but I discovered by accident this year that now we just pick kids at random for this honour. I told you any student could do it!

The Cult of the Headteacher

Like any school, XP's culture is only as strong as those that hold it. So what happens if our leadership changes, for whatever reason?

How does XP stay XP without the two people that have defined what it is, the most?

This is a problem for many schools, and it has given rise to the 'Cult of the Headteacher' where the individual is seen as the most important reason a school is how it is.

Many schools have seen, for good or bad, that a change in the Headteacher totally changes the fortunes of the school.

It has shifted the focus onto who is important, rather than what is important. This is often because the convention is to define a 'vision' for the school, and often this vision 'belongs' to someone, normally the Headteacher. When a new Headteacher comes along, they implement a new vision. Theirs.

XP has never been about one relatively small school in Doncaster; it is about not only changing how we teach our children, but how our children can reach their true potential. XP is not about the legacy of Andy and Gwyn; it is about the legacy of our students. And importantly, XP is not defined by a vision. It is based on design principles.

Being mindful of succession planning at the early stage of conception of the school, we took this opportunity to build in process and structure to ensure the culture of XP is situated centrally within the governance of the school, and that this approach is understood and implemented by all stakeholders:

1 **Cement the design principles at the highest point of governance by:**

   A The design principles being tightly defined in terms of 'what they look like'

   B Members of the Trust and Directors of the board all signing up to this, and being the custodians of our culture

2 **Judge the performance of the school by:**

   A Identifying Key Performance Indicators (KPIs) based on the design principles

   B The Board of Directors continual monitoring of the school against these KPIs

3 **Build leadership capacity within all stakeholders by:**

   A Governance committees creating Working Groups made from appropriate stakeholders including governors, staff, students, parents, the wider community and experts

   A The Working Groups carrying out action research to measure the performance against the KPIs based on our design principles

This creates 'distributed leadership' through all stakeholders as they:

- use their **voice,**
- show **ownership,**
- take **responsibility,**
- be **accountable,** and
- ensure **transparency**

This strategy for succession planning allows us to inevitably step back and for others to take on and grow into their leadership roles without the essence of the school being weakened or diluted.

Ultimately, it is hoped that some of our students will learn to be teachers and return to the school to become the future custodians of XP.

This is when Andy and I can retire.

But we won't.

Perception is reality

This little saying, 'perception is reality', reminds us that the truth of a situation is always from the perception of the person looking at it, and therefore, more than one 'truth' can exist at the same time.

If you see a situation, that's where you see it from, your perception. If you don't know that other things have happened to alter the 'truth', your truth stays the same.

This is a point about really good communication.

Any organisation IS communication.

How well we communicate is a measure of how good our organisation is.

Communication to parents is a good example. Most parents get most of their communication from their children. Parents are more than likely to believe their children. Therefore a parent's perception of your school is likely to be defined by their children, not your staff, unless you put energy into your communication.

We put energy into this by teachers and Crew leaders adding blog posts to our website every week, ensuring our parents know what is happening within our school. We feed back individually by 'making deposits' with parents. Before we send any letters out to parents, for instance, for poor attendance, we ensure we have contacted them in person first. The letter is just formal confirmation of any intervention we will put in place.

We say that parents should have 'no alarms, and no surprises'.

When we talk about a situation, we often say, 'my perception is this, am I right?', allowing others to clarify situations from their point of view.

This is important because, as people, we react to situations depending on our perception of it, because we believe it to be true. It is important to remember the complexity of a people-based solution to make great decisions.

Painting White Walls

When my house was being built, I was watching our painter do something I couldn't. We had decided to keep things simple, and paint all our walls white. And we have a lot of walls.

I like to work really hard at solving problems and getting them into place, but when I've done it once or twice, I find it boring having to do the same thing over and over again.

I would have loved to have sorted all the painting equipment out, and worked out how to paint straight lines and stop any drips, but after a few walls, I would have lost the will to live.

I saw our painter do something and I was curious. Every now and again, he'd stop. He'd put his stuff down, stretch and take a sip of tea and just stand there for a few seconds, before he picked up his stuff and carried on.

He did this like a machine throughout the house, and he was always looking happy and fulfilled in the knowledge that he was doing a good job.

I talked to him about it, and I told him I couldn't do what he did. He then told me his trick. He didn't see the whole job as a massive, overwhelming thing that never seemed to get any smaller. The reason he stopped every ten or so minutes is because he set himself a target to cover so much of the wall. An area he could do within ten minutes or so. Then when he had done it, he made sure he took a step back, and he admired his handiwork.

Teaching is so intense, that sometimes days just go missing.

We have to go slow to go fast.

Set targets and make sure we complete them before we move on. Have we actually done what we're supposed to have done? If we have, let's admire that for a little while before setting the next target.

When things seem like an overwhelming job, we must break them down into smaller parts, work out the most important thing to do next, and do that.

In our action plans, we may have big things to do that stretch over years, and we may or may not end up doing them, so we break stuff down and we look at each eight week term and ask ourselves, what can we do in the next six weeks? And then we do those things. If something takes more than six weeks, we break it down into smaller tasks and do them.

We have to remind ourselves to stand back and take a sip of tea and admire our work before we move on.

To ensure rigour, make things public

At HTH, the thing that sorts everything out in the end is the public exhibition. Students succeed and fail and have to answer for themselves. These exhibitions are also a measure of the teachers.

We make our kids do this, and what's good enough for our kids is good enough for us. So we make things public too when we're expected to do things.

We do Jeff's Law and Toby's Law in public (that is, in front of all our staff). We share all our planning and resources in public.

We say 'DONE' is a sacred word. Things are only done when they are done. It is binary.

When we do this, everyone knows what is expected of them, because it matters to them what other people think. They seek out support and challenge to ensure this. They welcome critique.

Then on the exhibition night (or in staff Crew), it becomes a public celebration.

"Oh, you did it that way, great! I need to do that next time"

"Yeah, I didn't quite nail that part, so I've changed it to this."

We celebrate getting things done and we get better.

Think tanks and action helicopters

You are what you do, not what you say.

The human sport of talking about stuff is an intoxicating ego massage. Yet a whole industry is built upon this.

People form think tanks to inform policy, while the government changes regularly and the Secretary of State even more so.

Millions of pounds is spent on research that doesn't show or mean anything, or worse, creates a headline for an ideology.

At XP, if we want to think about something, we form a working group. That working group will either end up doing something or decide not to.

Our working groups are action helicopters and they blow up think tanks.

Our school is our book on how to do school, and the source of our real evidence.

Don't make like a banana

Whoever thought that the way to get something important done, like learn something, is by splitting the task into one hour a week chunks, is a banana head.

The way to get lots of important things done is to work out what is the most important thing and do that. Then do the next thing. Then…

Say, *"this is really important, so we need to get it done, so let's spend [half a day / a day / two days / a week / a term] getting it done."*

Your timetable and staffing model is not king. Do not be dictated to by logistics. Get things done. Decide what's important and do it.

Don't make like a banana, and split. Shape the timetable to your will. Get staff as productive as possible.

Some examples:

We spent a whole term with Year 10 getting their Creative Craft VCert done. The teacher leading this had already started a new Expedition, but the massive amount of work the students had produced needed assessing. He took three days out of school to get that sorted.

This is much more productive than doing 'creative' one hour a week for two years and then waiting a couple of terms for the teacher to assess the portfolios in dribs and drabs.

It was done, and the teacher could focus fully on the new Expedition (and he caught up because the other teachers had taught their bit while he was out of school, so he took some of their timetabled sessions when he got back - so what's the cost / risk?)

It sounds so sensible to do things this way, but people get scared – so what's the cost / risk?

Be a punk and break things to fix them and make them better.

Offices are places where people go to die

Depending on staff roles, we all have a space to put our 'stuff'.
For teachers and learning coaches that looks like a 50cm wide area
of a workbench with room under it for either drawers or boxes and
possibly shelving above it. For admin staff, that's generally a desk
and some drawers.

Every other space is shared. Stores, classrooms, open plan working
areas and quiet rooms. Quiet rooms can be booked for meetings or
interventions or just a space to work uninterrupted.

Teachers don't have classrooms assigned to them. While most
teachers predominantly work in the same classroom, they are stewards,
not owners.

This isn't a fancy modern way of working – it is born out of rattling
around a school with space that is slowly filling up, and working out
what works best and what we need.

Andy used to have an office but he moved out because he didn't need it.

I've never had one. I find that when I work in an office, I get distracted
by the loneliness and the lack of accountability of having people around
you. Stuff gets collected, things fester and the next thing you know,
twenty years has gone by. Then you die.

We've all seen the grand offices that some Heads have. What a waste
of space. If books are any good, they should be in the library, not on a
shelf in an office that belongs to someone. Files and folders should be
in the cloud or the bin – depending on whether they are useful or not.

Transient stuff that you are given, or are actually referencing can fit in
your base, until you finish with it and put it somewhere useful, or deem
it not useful and bin it.

Offices stink of hierarchy, or length of time in service... and death.

Purge them and make them useful again.

What's in a word? Everything[10]

Words that supposedly describe our practice but don't:

- Progressive
- Innovative
- Child-centred
- Hands on
- Small
- Loose
- Project-based learning?
- Alternative

Words that supposedly describe other schools, but don't:

- Traditional
- Normal
- Big
- Strict
- Mainstream

Phrases that don't mean anything:

- I don't have time
- I need to cover...

One of our design principles is 'Language is our culture'. Our language defines us, and we're really careful how we use it. We define words carefully, we don't use certain words, and correct people when they do. We create phrases that we all understand the purpose of.

This book is full of them.

Do you have the time?

If a task takes 30 minutes and it needs to be done in 10 minutes, then okay – you don't have time to do it. But most of the time (-nice!), we say, *"I haven't got the time to..."*, when we actually mean, *"it is not important enough for me to do"*.

This can be done subconsciously, or flippantly, or dismissively.

---

10 Chris Coady told me this. I don't know where he got it from.

At XP, we ask our staff to have meaningful discussion around the importance of things to prioritise our work effectively. We know we all have the same amount of time as each other - there's twenty four hours in a day for everyone - and we just need to decide how we spend that time. These discussions lead to practices of productivity and workload, and we often refer to perceived urgency versus the important things.

Jeff's Law is one result of this, where an Expedition cannot start until the correct level of planning is achieved.

We all appreciate the intense nature of teaching, and the drive to be in front of kids doing stuff. But we must always ensure the stuff we are doing is the right stuff, and if we have to stop being in front of kids to do this, then we absolutely must.

Fear and Ego

Don't not do anything just because of your fear.
Don't just do something because of your ego.

Fear
We often talk about risks and how we can mitigate those risks, or whether the risk is worth the reward, but fear is being scared to try something in case it fails. We don't say failure is good, because it's not. Not at the time anyway. You can learn from failure, but y'know... try not to if you can help it.

But don't be scared of failure. Know the risk and try for the pay off. Everything can be fixed anyway.

Ego
Education is something more important than you. Err.... and me.

It's great to have something bigger and more important than yourself. A moral imperative. A noble mission.

The culture of 'my worksheet is better than your worksheet' - The cult of the headteacher - get a knighthood or die trying.

Arrggh! Let our weakness be our virtue. Try humility. We have. We're very good at it. We have very big humility. Much bigger than yours. We're the most humble people in the world. Not you.

Duck and cover

Teachers often use the term 'to cover', to relate to 'covering the curriculum'. In a recent staff Crew, we talked about what that actually meant. The problem being that teachers sometimes get into a bidding war of how much time they need to cover their part of the curriculum, with the outcome being that they need 'as much time as possible'.

There are a number of aspects to explore here.

One is that I don't believe any non-prescriptive curriculum is designed to the hour/day/academic calendar even though they have suggested or minimum (?!) teaching hours. It's just stuff you have to know to pass an exam.

Another is that 'to cover' should not mean - *'I have to speak this out loud in front of all my students, or they won't know it'.* When we discussed it, we came up with the notion that 'to cover' actually meant, *'I need to know that my students know...'* - and when you say it in these terms, you can suffix this with, *'so I am going to...'*

Things get more complex when you know that different students have different capabilities, capacities and motivation. Some students would successfully pass their GCSEs if you gave them a high quality text book and told them they had a test in two years. Some need much more help than this!

Ask yourself, *"how would I pass a GCSE?"* Most would answer like this:

- Get the specification from the examination board website
- Collate some resources (a high quality textbook, maybe some wider resources from the internet)
- Get all the past papers available
- Work through them until you have model answers, referring to the assessor's reports

Do not be the gatekeeper to this knowledge for your students. When it comes to coverage, uncover the curriculum first!

Then think about how you want to spend your time. By talking through facts? Or by giving nuanced feedback?

We need to think deeply about the most effective ways to ensure our students know how to do things, not just scramble to have more time with them.

Fail faster

Sometimes you feel you should challenge someone, but you feel you need them to do something, and you feel that if you challenge them, they will react badly. That is exactly why you should challenge them.

If there's something you need to do, but you don't know how it will work out, the danger is to procrastinate and drag out the issue while you attempt miserably at trying to find some other way round, but you can't and the thing gets worse the more you leave it.

If you feel you need to challenge something. **Do it faster.**

If you feel you need to abandon something. **Do it faster.**

It will work out one way or another.

I have seen so many times, people being challenged and then they react positively to that challenge, because there is support as well. The people who don't react positively – well, you don't want them around anyway do you? – It was never going to work.

Remember – everything can be fixed. Don't keep flogging a dead horse.

Fail faster.

Order! Order!

A lot of schools are modelled on creating order.

What if we embrace that learning is messy and chaotic (we are people right?)

What if we base our school model on making good decisions in chaos? – allowing people to act in complex ways and harness the power of the tornado to sit in the eye of the storm.

To tap into the child's innate sense of fairness, and allow them to buy into a shared culture – a community – a model of society – that they choose to belong to.

Everything can be fixed

Procrastination is evil. It saps time, energy and confidence.

If you feel you can make an informed decision, make it. Try it. Everything can be fixed. It's your decision - you own it.

I was building my house, and we were half way through, and building a home for your family is extremely stressful as there are a million details and you so desperately want to get everything right, because when you build a house, you only get one shot don't you?

I was procrastinating like this when my builder said to me, *"Why don't you try it? Everything can be fixed..."*

Then he added... *"It just takes time and money."*

Then he added... *"What's the worse that can happen? It all goes wrong, we knock the house down and we start again."*

Everything can be fixed.

The 'Muttley' effect

"Ok, so we're all agreed, yes? We're going to have X done by Y...?"

"Yeh, yeh, yeh, yeh, yeh"

Then at Y you find out they've:

A Not done X

B Done Z instead and not told you

Sometimes staff can be perceived as being totally unprofessional. Like Muttley, you perceive them as your trusted companion, you set them off to do something and it ends in total disaster. As a leader (or somebody that needs to ensure things get done), you have to ask yourself if you've done your best to ensure things will get done.

This is the idea that you are the 'backstop' - if the ball goes flying off, it's you that needs to go after it and pick it up. The truth with most teachers is that they have a million and one things in their heads, and we all know how intense teaching is. They are not experts in project management and getting things done. It is a craft that needs working on, that needs to be learnt, and if you want your teachers to be good at it, you need to think about how to teach these skills.

At XP, we focus on 'getting things done' and we put protocols and support in place to help staff to achieve this.

To avoid the 'Muttley effect', we do things such as:

- Non-negotiable expectations (e.g. Jeff's Law/Toby's Law)
- Regular public check-ins
- Transparent, shared planning documents
- 'It's ok to fail... as long as you tell someone' policy
- Everything can be fixed - it just takes time and resource
- High expectations with support and challenge

If we do all the above, everything will be great, won't it?

Yeh, yeh, yeh, yeh, yeh...

Knights with shining torches

We don't want knights in shining armour. People stepping in to fix other people's mistakes makes the problem worse.

> A difficulty is a light.
> An insurmountable difficulty is a sun.
>
> **Paul Valery**

As a LEADER at XP, I will:

• Use my voice

• Show ownership

• Take responsibility

• Be accountable

• Ensure transparency

Don't manage a problem. Solve it.

When you decide how to solve a problem, one of the things you can decide to do, is nothing.

If you can't solve it, fail faster.

Do not worship false gods

The people we need to respect the most are the people who work in and with schools that produce tangible success.

We do not need to respect people who earn a living spreading the word according to them, their friends who do the same, and people you have not heard of.

We call them 'edutainers'.

They play on your fears, quoting people you have not heard of, and say things like, *"Oh you must have read [made up name] - oh you haven't? Oh you must... you see, they say.... Blah blah blah... Have you read the research paper by Dr No? No? Oh no!"*

They often put down the latest thing everyone is talking about, often by just saying the name of it in a sarcastic voice to garner a few nervous laughs from the audience, then they fill you with their empty delights, with sprinkles of humour, and then we all applaud and feed their ego.

This was all we had to put up with and it was limited to 'INSET' days – until twitter and blogs arrived. Now we have to suffer the rise of the celebrity teacher. When celebrity teachers get enough followers on Twitter, they stop teaching and become edutainers.

Or, worse still, they stay as teachers but can't possibly teach very well as they are tweeting every second of every day. Stop it.

We need to respect each other and visit our schools and work together on meaningful and purposeful projects that produce tangible outcomes.

You are what you do, not what you say.

We don't need them.

My worksheet is better than your worksheet

There is one thing in the world of education that I find absolutely crazy, and that is our inability to share.

It is 2019, we have something called 'the internet', and I ask, *"Where is the website that everyone can go to, to learn maths?"* - Where there are high quality videos, explaining each concept, with loads of example questions to practise and worked out answers for those examples. The map of the layered elements, the log in so you can check your progress, the teacher screen so you can see your student progress and can prompt them, give them bespoke tasks, send prompts to parents to help them know what they can do to help etc etc etc...???

Yes, I know there are commercial products out there, and we use them. Yes, I know there are scattered resources across the internet that vary in quality, but why is there not a free resource, perhaps funded by our government who supposedly want our kids to learn maths, that helps all our children for free?

How many maths teachers are there in the UK? Could we like, not teach maths for one week, get all the good maths teachers together and create something amazing for our children?

The whole basis of how we learn is how we share, yet there is a culture of thinking that my worksheet is better than your worksheet, and one day, my worksheet will make me a millionaire!

Apparently, a long time ago, someone called George Bernard Shaw said, *"If you have an apple and I have an apple and we exchange these apples then you and I will still each have one apple. But if you have an idea and I have an idea and we exchange these ideas, then each of us will have two ideas."*

How much time do you as an individual teacher spend creating resources?

What commercial companies do is this. They go, hmmm... there's not a very good history book that helps kids get through the history exam, so we'll pay a load of decent history teachers to create a book, then we'll sell it to everyone.

What we need to do is this. Go, hmmm... there's not a very good history book that helps kids get through the history exam, so let's get together to create an online repurposable bank of resources, and share it with everyone.

For free. And if we don't, then we don't love our children enough.

I'm not naive. I know the commercial aspects to this problem. And this is a stark example of how money and individualism and short term pressures are stopping us progressing.

I have no problem at all with people who have made great resources and made money from this. That's great, and like I said, we use these resources in our schools.

I just can't understand this apparent human condition that stops us all sharing things, when this is the business we are in.

Ironically, the best people I have met that are great at sharing are our good friends from the USA, the country famed for making money out of anything. The amount of grace and good will and their ability to share with us has been phenomenal.

If we have achieved anything at all, it is because we are standing on the shoulders of these giants that have shared everything with us, and wished us the best with our moral imperative - our noble mission.

This is a small part of us doing the same.

Thank you.

If it's good enough for the kids...

...it's good enough for us.

We started our school with this mantra. We decided that our kids should start school with an Outward Bound experience, so that's what we did as staff.

When we design Expeditions, we do the project first. If we are expecting our kids to do it, then we should do it. If we're bored when we're doing this, then our kids will be bored! We don't want to be hypocrites now, do we?

As we've grown our school, we've not gone further away from this, in fact, we've come closer. Our next move is to peer assess ourselves as staff against our HoWLs. The same HoWLs that our kids use to assess themselves.

There's nothing more powerful to demonstrate this than our staff induction.

Staff induction

On the first day of school, our students board a coach and set off on an Outward Bound adventure. Here they begin to explore the concept of Crew, start to acquire our language and are introduced to our Character Traits and Habits of Work and Learning. So what do we do when new staff start at the school?

Exactly the same.

We appoint our staff early so that they can start early at the school, usually at the start of June. This gives new staff a chance to immerse themselves in our culture, ethos and practices so that when they start to lead Crew and teach Expeditions, they are ready.

The first part of induction is indeed similar to an outward bound experience. Staff who invariably do not know each other, and have different interests, board a bus and head out to the wilderness as a Crew. During this time they take part in a series of challenges where they have to work together and support each other to answer the guiding question, 'What is Crew?' Staff have a challenging, shared experience and they are allowed to reflect on both who they are as a person and who they are as an educator. This is a very powerful experience and the group of staff very quickly heighten their understanding of our values and often for the first time in years reflect on their own characters, including their strengths and weaknesses.

When staff return to school they are 'Crew'. They have shared their personal reflections on who they are through Crew and have supported each other through those challenging experiences creating friendships, trust, and most of all, profoundly deep and unbreakable bonds – just like the kids do in Wales and bring back into school.

The next stage of induction builds on the outdoor experience and applies the previous learning back into the classroom, making the requisite link between fieldwork and Expeditions, as staff begin an Expedition 'slice' – a Learning Expedition condensed into a short space of time.

In the next week to ten days, staff are led through an Expedition. They actively engage, like students, in the anatomy of an Expedition so that they have a visceral experience of how we deliver the curriculum and reflect as teachers how this would impact on their pedagogy and practice.

In short, staff embark on immersion, a guiding question is revealed that they must grapple with, they work through case studies with the support of experts, take their learning outside the classroom through fieldwork and they culminate their Expedition 'slice' with a product and with a presentation of their learning to an authentic audience (usually the kids!). The Expedition is cross subject and highly challenging to allow staff to really feel what it is like to go beyond what is comfortable, understand learning from a learner's perspective and unpack this as a teacher.

After the 'slice', new staff are then tasked with preparing a speech that outlines how they have changed as an educator over the past few weeks. Once completed, staff need to be ready to deliver this to an audience of colleagues and invited guests. This is one of the most breathtaking and emotional events I've ever had the privilege to experience. Staff reveal their learning and growth honestly and with great courage. We are stripped back so that we can remember why we became educators and why this is the most noble of professions.

The following weeks allow staff to get to know other staff and students, buddy up, visit sessions, observe how protocols are used, experience Crew first hand, take part in Book Clubs and start to plan the next Expedition as part of an Expedition team. This development process continues throughout their time at XP through the rigorous collaborative design of our curriculum.

Our staff induction process is a powerful and necessary experience. Staff not only reconfigure how and what they might teach through an Expedition, they also immerse themselves in the culture of the school. How we learn and who we are, are indelibly linked. Through creating beautiful work we become better people and the induction process allows staff to realise and recognise this.

The value of this approach over the coming months and years is of inestimable worth as we begin the process of growing great people, teachers, learners and leaders.

In our local context of Doncaster, which is currently the second highest excluding district in the UK, we have the highest attendance and lowest exclusion rate.

We have only permanently excluded one child in our history (our first year), and we shouldn't have had to.

We have a roughly average demographic.

We're doing something right, that works with our kids in our context.

Ofsted describes the behaviour of our students as 'exemplary', but it isn't all the time. Sometimes they drive us bonkers and sometimes they make us cry. In a good way.

Beyond the mistakes of our children that sometimes leave us confounded, I have seen behaviours in our children that I never thought possible. The compassion, courage and integrity of children when given a voice and a safe environment is wonderous. They put us adults to shame. Visitors are often moved to tears when watching our community meetings, where anyone can appreciate others, apologise for their actions and make pledges to put things right, and make stands for our character traits. While we have no religious ethos, a visitor once described us as 'the most christian' school they had ever visited. I think this is because the compassion we show each other, alongside our tough and high expectations, is palpable in the atmosphere.

The danger of an observer coming into our school and experiencing the community meetings, active and engaged lessons, is that they think, *"what lovely children!"* - and they are! But what they don't see is the incredible amount of work we put in to ensure this is how our children behave. It doesn't just happen.

These are random kids from Doncaster. Just like random kids from anywhere.

Every child is different, with different starting places, different social privileges, life experiences and support networks.

They look to us for guidance, to model our character traits and habits of work and learning, to meet them where they are, to get them to where they need to be.

However, as adults, we are flawed. We judge children, and we judge groups of children. We name the observed behaviours of children as if this is what they are. When we judge groups of children, we dehumanise them.

As adults, we know that the behaviours of children differ, depending on their environment and the adults that are in those environments. We know that these children grow up despite their experience of school and become business leaders, builders, nurses, plumbers, electricians, shop workers, road sweepers, bartenders... all these people that we rely upon every day of our everyday lives. Yet we judge children as being 'naughty' or groups of children as being 'annoying'.

We are the adults here, yet sometimes we forget that children, like adults, make mistakes and they need to be given the chance to put things right, not labelled forever more and consigned to a cycle of self-depreciation.

We need to show compassion. And we need to skilfully change our environments and actions to meet them where they are, redefine purpose and norms, and give them the foundation to build up again.

We need to remind ourselves that, yes, children could be behaved wonderfully for us, but we can change our behaviours too.

A few anecdotes help me remember this.

It is straightforward to see a class of children behaving really well, and then later in the same day, with a different teacher, seeing them not behaving, and to surmise that the difference is the teacher. To an observer, they might see the first class and think, 'what lovely children'. But if the same observer saw the second lesson in isolation, they would think, 'what terrible children'.

Andy has an even more powerful anecdote. He tells a story about a tough 'bottom set' he taught English. After a few weeks, he had got to know them, and they were great for him. He's a great teacher. Then one day, he had to cover a Maths lesson. He turned up to the maths classroom and it was the same group of kids. He handed out the maths worksheets, but the kids were all over the place. Andy tried to remind them that they were with him, but they were having none of it.

Andy, fed up with the situation, rounded them up and took them to his english classroom. They came in, settled down and he handed out the same worksheets, and they just got on with it.

That would have confused the observer judging the behaviour of the kids!

The point about judging groups of children is a similar adult issue. *"Class 3 were terrible last lesson. They just wouldn't settle down. Good luck to you for next lesson..."* etc. We hear stuff like this all the time in 'teacherland'. At XP we challenge this... *"What, all the class? Even Emily..? No...? Jack...? No...? Oh, who then...? So just two kids then. Ok I'll have a word with them before they come into the classroom."*

As adults, we judge groups of people all the time and then label them with behaviours. If you live in the same country, have the same sex, the same political view, the same skin colour, the same religion, then apparently you are all connected and therefore behave in the same way. Well, we all know that is rubbish, so we need to stop doing the same to groups of children.

Some schools take the position that we are the adults and you are the children, so you must respect us, because we know better than you, and we are better than you. You only have to look around the world to how adults behave in the most senior, privileged roles in society to know that this is also nonsense.

If we take our kids on fieldwork, and they act up, the first things we ask are: Did we circle up and establish the shared purpose? Did we agree norms? Did we agree consequences of poor behaviours? How did we carry out these pledges on the fieldwork? What could we have done differently as adults?

For clarity, this isn't to take the blame away from children. We do this as well as holding our students to account for their actions. They reflect on what they've done, and they pledge how they can put things right and their peers hold them accountable for this, with us, as adults, ensuring this happens.

We are the adults. Remember this. Always.

Children, like adults, make mistakes. Put them right.

The vast majority of kids have an innate sense of fairness built into them. We build on this, give them a shared vocabulary and a voice. I would argue that we don't teach them how to be. It is within them already.

Spectrums of approach

There seems to be spectrums of approach that schools can be identified along

Expression and conformity

Giving children the space to explore and express who they are / We are the adults, you will do as we say as we know best.

Equality and equity

Treat all the kids exactly the same with consistency / Treating kids according to need.

Punitive and restorative

Punish kids with menial tasks for doing something wrong / Allowing children to put their mistakes right.

Reactive and proactive

Reacting to poor behaviour / Proactively promoting good behaviour.

These aren't opposite, mutually exclusive things, but you can use these spectrums to identify where you are along them, and maybe adjust approach, depending on what you want your outcomes to be.

Expression and conformity

Respectful personal expression

At XP, we welcome personal expression. We have a dress code, not a school uniform, and we don't mind kids having long or short hair, or colour. Extreme haircuts, at our school at least, don't positively correlate to academic underachievement.

That doesn't mean we allow kids to wear anything. Our dress code is, 'Dress appropriately and modestly', and we expand what that means on our website: **www.xptrust.org/dress-code**

We use sayings like, *"If you can see up it, down it or through it, it's not appropriate"*.

This doesn't result in a horrible fashion show. Actually, the reality is that most of our students wear jeans and t-shirts. Girls tend to be more imaginative and look great. Some push the make up and jewellery, but not many, and I must say they look a whole lot better to me than the usual St Trinians line up I observe at other schools, or indeed, trussed up, miserable, 'I'm being forced to wear these horrible clothes' expressions we also see.

They look like themselves. They express who they are respectfully.

We don't spend inordinate amounts of time telling kids to straighten their ties all day, every day either (how much time and money does that save?) You can't tell which kids are rich and which are poor. Most of the time, kids rock up in normal kid clothes, which are appropriate. Rarely, we have conversations about what 'modest' means and what is appropriate. We've never had to send a kid home. Rarely we have had to ask some children not to wear expensive jewellery or less revealing tops (eg crop top) for the next day, and they do. We have had one request to wear jewellery for a religious nature, which we've said ok to.

We have sometimes joked that we could have a 'uniform day', like other schools have 'non-uniform days'. But we've never done it...

I hated school uniform, and I hated the school for forcing me to wear it. I thought it was stupid and pointless. I still do.

I overheard a girl say once, *"I wish we had a uniform"* and I replied by saying, *"what's stopping you from wearing one?"*. Her real issue was that she felt she'd not got any different clothes to wear at the weekend. I think that's an easy one to solve! We have branded clothing anyway, which some kids and staff wear, so they don't have to think about their selection.

How important this is to our culture and behaviour, I've no idea – I've visited great schools that have uniform – but it feels right to me.

Personalisation

The main way we encourage our children to explore and express who they are though, is through their work. This is what we mean by personalisation. Their work on authentic products allows them to express who they are while creating beautiful work. As a result, they achieve academically. It matters to them. It motivates them. They strive to be the best version of themselves and present that to others.

Voice

We give our students voice. Interestingly, we don't have a school council, which gives the chosen few the voice. Instead, we have Crew and community meetings where all students can express who they are through praise, apology, pledges and stands.

Crew is once a day. Community meetings happen whole school every week, and year groups meet once every two weeks normally.

Voice in Crew happens when we do 'check-ins'. We circle up and go round everyone and we check-in. This can be different things, but mainly something like, *"tell me one significant thing that happened to you over the weekend"*. It lets all students talk about something with their peers and their Crew Leader, their trusted adult (normally a teacher, but sometimes a learning coach / teaching assistant).

Crew is 45 minutes every morning from 8:30-9:15 and pastorally prepares our students for the day. We do many activities in Crew, including academic Crew. Our students describe it as being like a family in school, a home from home. We hold each other to account for the pledges we make, and we support and challenge appropriately guided by the Crew leader.

Crew is in year groups, and is 12 or 13 students to one adult. We have Crew buddies so we can do vertical Crew activities when appropriate.

It's amazing how disparate children grow to bond with unlikely friendships. They achieve more because of their differences.

All our kids do Duke of Edinburgh Bronze (in year 9) and Silver (in year 10). We have a +90% success rate at Bronze and +80% at Silver. Their Bronze is done in Crew groups. At silver, they can choose (or negotiate!) their groups.

In community meetings, as well as teacher input similar to a conventional 'assembly', we use a 'catchbox', a throwable microphone, to allow our students voice. Here, all our students and staff can make appreciations, they can apologise and make pledges, and they can make stands. This is all done respectfully, and is never forced. The children want to use their voice. They feel safe.

Appreciations always outweigh anything else, and if a student makes a pledge, their Crew will hold them to account.

It is in community meetings where I have seen and heard things I never thought I would in a school environment. I have heard a year 7 girl hold a year 10 boy to account for lack of stewardship because he threw an empty box of Tic-Tacs at the bin in the playground, but it didn't go in, and he didn't pick it up. She said he didn't show stewardship. She didn't know the name of the year 10 boy, as she had only been at the school a few weeks. The year 10 boy, without prompt, stood up and admitted it was he who committed this heinous crime, and he pledged to show more stewardship.

Ridiculous, I know. But it happened. And it happened with normal kids from Doncaster. The laddie in question was from Mexborough, and certainly not a middle-class background, so this idea of demographic being an overriding factor is not visible at our school. It is certainly a factor, but not an overriding one. Culture is king.

I have seen visitors in tears because they witness the compassion, honesty and courage of genuine student voice. Again, the danger is, they walk away thinking the kids that go to XP are extremely well behaved.

Shared expectations

From the first day at school, where our students find themselves on an Outward Bound residential, we talk constantly and consistently about our Character Traits and Habits of Work and Learning (Our HoWLs).

This is our conformity. We expect all of us to show Courage, Respect, Craftsmanship & Quality, Compassion and Integrity. These are not just words on walls, we talk about these traits, and what they look like, sound like and feel like, every day.

We expect each other to Work Hard, Get Smart and Be Kind, and again, we break down what these look like in context of our school, so we can talk specifically about issues and break down those barriers to learning.

These expectations are very hard for children to argue against. They build on their innate sense of fairness, and our students hold each other to account using this shared language. It allows them to be specific and focus on helpful solutions... *"So, how can Billy show more compassion in this situation? What does that look like?"*

When students make mistakes, we use our character traits and HoWLs to unpack the situation, allowing students to reflect on their actions, how they could have done things differently, and work out how to put their mistakes right.

Equality and equity

"That isn't fair!"

How many times have we, as teachers, dished out a consequence to a student and heard these three words...?

Treating all our students the same, consistently, with the same consequences for the same behaviours is the Holy Grail for many behaviour policies. Creating taxonomies of behaviours, codes to assign, consequences and interventions, posters for clarity, rules and acronyms can be a joy for some.

Parents and students accept and understand the rulebook. As a computer programmer, it's easy: IF A, THEN B

This is equality.

If all our children were the same, it would be the perfect approach. The problem is, they aren't. They are pretty much all different. Like adults, we act and react in different ways.

Equity takes into account the different needs of children and adults. Some of us need different things. When you think about disabilities, it is obvious. We need to be treated differently to be treated 'fairly'.

Most of this comes through relationships and knowing your children well. You know what makes them tick, how to coerce them into showing great learning dispositions. Some need a quiet word. Some need a sharp look. Some need reminding you have their dad's mobile number on speed dial.

In our mixed ability classes, differentiation is a highly visible version of equity working well to get everyone up their respective mountains.

When kids have special educational needs (SEN) that sometimes display as poor behaviours, we need to learn as a community to be tolerant while at the same time knowing that certain behaviours are not acceptable and that they have consequences.

We are still learning how to be more equitable with the small number of children who struggle at our school, in our highly social environments, and I know we can get better, but we will endeavour to take the equitable route.

Equality and equity is a spectrum, and what I have seen is that equality has a heavy price to pay in regard to low income, low ability and children with SEN. Behaviour practices based on equality lets these children down.

Punitive and restorative

If a student has done something wrong, do we:

A Punish them with menial tasks so they don't do it again?

B Allow them to put their mistakes right?

We all know the conventional punitive tasks; staying in at break/lunch, doing lines, detention etc, but actually putting right what you've done can be a lot harder, authentic and can create a positive change more effectively.

Some students may need more support than others to see how, if they changed their behaviours, the outcome may have been different. Models, templates and social stories often help here.

Restorative consequences at XP go far beyond an apology, even a public one, and often result in community service, or extra responsibility.

Reactive and proactive

We all have high expectations and expect our students to model them. Do we react when they don't, or react when they do?

At XP, we talk about deposits and withdrawals. We make deposits when we catch students being good. We make contact with parents and make deposits with them too.

We do this at staff level too. It's part of making rigour a public celebration.

When we are praising our students (and staff) for great behaviours, it's much easier to make a withdrawal.

If we have been contacting our parents regularly with positive news and information, the time we need to phone and share some bad news, we have built up a relationship and trust. It is much more likely that parents trust the judgement of a teacher if they know they are seeing good things from their children as well as the not so good.

In Crew and community meetings, we make way more appreciations than apologies or stands.

In these areas of practice, they are not mutually exclusive, but spectrums.

Conformity	Expression
Equality	Equity
Punitive	Restorative
Reactive	Proactive

We recognise that most of the practices to the left are lower energy in terms of resource (time. effort. money), except maybe expression over conformity, but at XP, we choose to do much more of the practices to the right.

The main reason we do this is so that our students become our school, rather than just come to our school.

Schools that choose most of the practices on the left tend to have a high price to pay; Low attendance and high internal, fixed-term and permanent exclusions, which almost always equates to low income, low ability and children with SEN losing out.

This approach leaves schools with a less than comprehensive cohort, and a more conforming cohort which results in better academic progress with the cohort that is left. It also creates a business model that allows the monies saved to be funnelled upwards into leadership and away from the students.

Schools should reflect the society we want to live in.

How XP do 'behaviour'

We want our students to not just feel safe, but have a respectful voice. We do this through our 'teacher-led, student-engaged' way. We model it, we give ownership of it to our students. This isn't a 'done to' process, it is theirs. We just happen to have created and shaped it.

This is a logistical fly-through of how we create a positive and safe culture at XP.

Traditional character values

We have five character traits that we refer to all the time, every day in most lessons. These are:

Courage

- to put ourselves outside our comfort zone to develop and deepen our learning and character
- to have conviction in our thoughts and feelings and communicate them effectively
- to endeavour to succeed, even though there is a chance of failure

Respect

- to respect ourselves and others
- to work with others despite differences or difficulties
- to show consideration towards other people and our environment

Craftsmanship and Quality

- to always strive to create beautiful work
- to take time and effort to draft, redraft and critique our work
- to aim for a quality in our work that is indistinguishable from professionals

Compassion

- to show understanding, care, love and pride for ourselves and other people
- to be committed to contributing positively to our community
- to help others to achieve

Integrity

- to be self-motivated to achieve our best
- to build resilience, responsibility and a never give up attitude
- to recognise the reasons for failure and, as a result, enhance our chances for success

From our Year 6 induction until our students leave, we refer to these character traits in terms of what they look like, feel like and sound like.

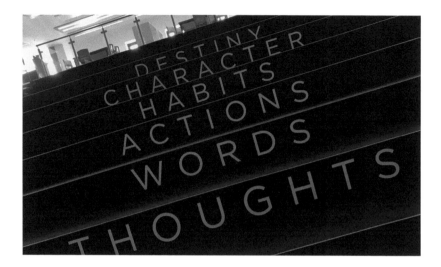

They are not words on walls, they are our common language to describe how our behaviours manifest and how we have grown as people.

While we could have used other words, such as resilience and honesty, we took inspiration from other schools, and drew big venn diagrams, and worked out how anything would fit into these five traits, so resilience could fit into courage, craftsmanship and integrity.

We worried that our children may not know the meaning of integrity, but then we remembered we were teachers, so maybe we could teach them what it meant. I heard a Year 7 student describe integrity as 'doing the right thing when no-one is looking'. This is an example of how this culture affects adults too. How many of us could do with reflecting on how we show integrity? Me, certainly. When, as adults, we talk about these traits day in, day out, we can't help but become infected by the same positive messages.

All, and I mean all, our students could not just recite our traits, but they can tell you what they look, sound and feel like, and they can give examples of when they have seen, heard and felt them.

These are traditional values that children find it hard to argue that they shouldn't show. Again, that innate sense of fairness allows us to start from these building blocks.

Habits of Work and Learning (HoWLs)

We say that our character traits manifest themselves in our habits of work and learning (which we call 'HoWLs'), which are:

Work Hard

- I arrive for each session on time and prepared.
- I participate fully and mindfully in every session.
- I complete all work in a timely manner to the best of my ability.

Get Smart

- I take responsibility for my learning by asking questions and seeking help when needed
- I assess my work based on established criteria and rubrics
- I welcome feedback and revise my work

Be Kind

- I communicate politely and kindly
- I work cooperatively with others
- I take care of resources and materials and act as a steward of our community

We adopted and adapted these from Springfield Renaissance School, Massachusetts, USA and King Middle School, Maine, USA.

Again, working hard to get smart while being kind is a simple and clear message of expectation which is extremely hard for children (and adults) to argue against. These aren't punitive, baseless 'school rules', they are fundamental and positive messages for success.

By starting from this point of expectations of character, we don't need loads of complex rules. We have simple rules. For instance, our IT policy is 'only use your devices for education use', because everything else is covered by our character traits.

We have discussions around this, and the grey areas that can emerge, and that is good! We want complex conversations. It enables our students to see how they fit, and how what we are asking is fair.

A narrative for success

Building onto our mission statement for our schools, 'Preparing our children to be successful in the modern world', we have a very simple narrative for success:

1 **Come to school, because every day at school matters.**

2 **Work hard**

3 **Get smart**

4 **Be kind**

5 **...and we will become a better person**

6 **...and we will create beautiful work**

7 **...and we will achieve academically**

I have numbered the list above, because this is in order of importance.

All the data we have ever captured shows this explicit correlation. The real evidence is in front of our eyes when we interact with our students.

The list above illustrates the bottom three things as being a consequence of the top four things.

It says that the most important intervention you can do for a child is to ensure they are at school in the first place.

Yet conventionally, attendance is something to be reported on, and an administration process of sending out letters of warning. The last thing most schools do is to call parents in, or 'Education Welfare Officers'. And of course, the fines. We have never sent a fine to a parent, yet we have the best attendance in our locale.

We have found that the only effective intervention to improve attendance is to build a personal, bespoke relationship with a family. We do this through Crew. One adult to twelve or thirteen students.

We focus relentlessly on attendance first. So in our weekly community meetings, we announce the week's attendance of each Crew, and this forms an attendance 'league' where Crew get points for coming higher than other Crews. Like a football league, if a Crew comes equal to another in terms of percentage attendance, the number of late marks is the 'goal difference'.

This weekly focus means that any Crew can win any week. It creates a fun, competitive purpose for positive peer pressure, and it is celebrated every week.

Academic interventions

As you can see from the list, achieving academically is a consequence of all the other things above it. Yet like most secondary schools, we have concentrated almost wholly on directed academic interventions to raise achievement / improve progress. We now believe that this is extremely ineffective, because they often come too late.

As we were reflecting on this narrative and connecting our thoughts to interventions, we found a blog post by Becky Allen:

https://rebeccaallen.co.uk/2018/12/01/poor-attainment-data-often-comes-too-late

> Attainment data is a lagged indicator that a student or staff member had a problem. Poor attainment data often comes too late. The trick is to sniff out the leading indicators that tell leaders where to step in before the damage is done.
>
> **Becky Allen**

This really resonated with us. Becky has way more data to analyse than us, and seems to know her onions. We seem to have come to the same conclusion with our one school data set, intuition and reflective practice.

If a student doesn't progress academically as expected, is it:

A because they don't understand some knowledge or concept?

or

B because they weren't at school, or they weren't working hard in that lesson, or getting smart, or even being kind?

We would say that it's more effective to look at all the (B) reasons before putting loads of energy into (A) as it will be more effective.

How much energy do we as professionals spend on analysing academic progress data, and how much of what we do from that positively impacts on our kids?

1 The student completes an assessed piece of work
2 The teacher marks all the classwork
3 The data is collected from a 'data drop'
4 Leadership analyse the data
5 Academic interventions are put in place

That's a lot of high cost energy put in to an intervention that is often too late to have any meaningful impact.

Compare that to the energy we spend on ensuring kids are:

1 Here in the first place
2 Working hard
3 Getting smart
4 Being kind

Most of the above is quality first teaching, and to the skilled teacher, is low energy with massive impact.

What if this information is collated every week, peer assessed and we are able to discuss it every day in Crew?

We are currently doing this, and it is having a much more significant effect in our classrooms than delayed academic interventions. We feel that by focusing on the most important things, the consequences pretty much look after themselves.

Here, we have collected the data on attendance, HoWLs and academic progress and publicly celebrated this in school, using it to visually demonstrate the narrative for success.

Y7/E25 Students who are smashing their MEGs
(achieving and surpassing MEGs in more than 3 subjects - **Data drop 1**)

	Attendance	Work Hard Average	Get Smart Average	Be Kind Average	English	History	Maths	Science
Dylan ap Harri	99%	3.3	3.3	3.5	Almost achieved MEG	Achieved MEG	Achieved above MEG	Achieved MEG
Lilly Cliff	100%	4.0	4.0	4.0	Significantly above MEG	Significantly above MEG	Significantly above MEG	Significantly above MEG
Faith Farmery	100%	3.5	3.5	3.5	Almost achieved MEG	Achieved MEG	Significantly above MEG	Achieved MEG
Ava Fletcher Bedford	100%	4.0	4.0	4.0	Achieved MEG	Achieved MEG	Achieved above MEG	Achieved MEG
Sam Fourie	100%	4.0	4.0	4.0	Almost achieved MEG	Achieved MEG	Achieved above MEG	Achieved above MEG
Charlotte Marsden	100%	4.0	4.0	4.0	Achieved above MEG	Achieved MEG	Significantly above MEG	Achieved MEG
Abigail Moore	100%	3.1	3.5	3.7	Significantly above MEG	Achieved above MEG	Almost achieved MEG	Achieved MEG
Zach Murray	100%	3.4	3.0	3.0	Achieved MEG	Achieved MEG	Achieved above MEG	Achieved above MEG
Nikodem Parzybut	100%	3.4	3.0	3.0	Achieved MEG	Achieved MEG	Achieved MEG	Achieved MEG
Charles Robinson	94%	4.0	4.0	4.0	Achieved MEG	Achieved MEG	Achieved above MEG	Achieved above MEG
Jessica Rollin	100%	3.7	4.0	4.0	Achieved MEG	Almost achieved MEG	Achieved above MEG	Achieved MEG
Dylan Smith	97%	4.2	4.0	4.0	Achieved MEG	Achieved MEG	Achieved above MEG	Achieved above MEG
Kristian Smith	100%	3.3	3.6	3.3	Significantly above MEG	Achieved above MEG	Achieved above MEG	Achieved MEG
Rosie Snow	100%	3.8	4.0	3.8	Achieved MEG	Achieved MEG	Achieved above MEG	Achieved MEG
Shanna Wallace	97%	3.0	3.3	3.5	Achieved above MEG	Achieved MEG	Achieved MEG	Achieved above MEG
Cerys May	97%	4.0	3.8	4.0	Achieved MEG	Almost achieved MEG	Achieved MEG	Achieved above MEG

In this display, we have collated just the average HoWLs of each Crew, to add an element of competition and positive peer pressure:

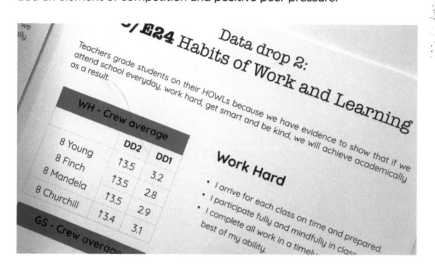

/ E24 Data drop 2:
Habits of Work and Learning

Teachers grade students on their HoWLs because we have evidence to show that if we attend school everyday, work hard, get smart and be kind, we will achieve academically as a result.

WH - Crew average	DD2	DD1
8 Young	↑3.5	3.2
8 Finch	↑3.5	2.8
8 Mandela	↑3.5	2.9
8 Churchill	↑3.4	3.1
GS - Crew average		

Work Hard

- I arrive for each class on time and prepared.
- I participate fully and mindfully in class.
- I complete all work in a timely best of my ability.

Pledge wall

The attendance and HoWLs data is collected every week and discussed in Crew. As a result, students make pledges, and their Crew hold them to account. When a Crew member fulfills their pledge, they are celebrated on our 'pledge wall'.

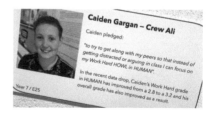

Caiden Gargan – Crew Ali

Caiden pledged:

"to try to get along with my peers so that instead of getting distracted or arguing in class I can focus on my Work Hard HOWL in HUMAN".

In the recent data drop, Caiden's Work Hard grade in HUMAN has improved from a 2.8 to a 3.2 and his overall grade has also improved as a result.

Year 7 / E25

Sami Fourie – Crew Turing

Sami has been a constant shining example in Crew Turing since starting here at XP East. He made a pledge to:

"contribute more in sessions at his SLC".

I have seen a vast improvement in his participation in class. He's also made gains in his grades, and has an exemplary set of HoWLs scores.

Beyond this, Sami is often appreciated for his compassion in helping and reminding others when they need support. We love having him around!

Year 7 / E25

In this example, Crew Finch were at the bottom of every HoWLs league table, averaging less than 3.0 (Secure), which is our minimum expected grade for HoWLs. Since this data drop, Angela (Crew Finch's Crew leader) posted this:

When hard work pays off

 By A Parker   26th March 2019

3.5	3.8	3.9	3.0	3.6	3.5	3.5	3.5	3.5	3.5
3.5	4.0	3.5	3.5	3.5	3.0	3.5	3.0	3.0	3.5
4.0	4.0	3.8	4.0	3.5	3.5	3.5	4.0	4.0	4.0
4.0	4.0	3.5	3.5	3.5	3.5	3.5	4.5	4.5	4.5
4.0	3.0	3.3	3.5	3.0	3.0	3.5	3.0	3.0	4.0
3.5	3.8	3.5	3.5	3.5	3.5	3.5	3.8	3.5	3.8
3.5	3.5	3.5	3.5	3.2	3.5	3.5	3.5	3.5	3.8

It might just look like rows of numbers to you, but to me it's proof that the work we've been doing in Academic Crew around our habits of work and learning is paying off!

I've had a sneak peek at the latest assessment data for Crew Finch, and I'm pleased to say that there has been a massive improvement in the grades awarded to our Crew members for getting smart, working hard and being kind across Humanities, Science and Maths. I'm also pleased to report that the Crew average in all areas has risen since the last data drop in November (assuming my maths is correct!)

I'm going to wait for Mr Portman's "big reveal" before posting our results, but let's just say it's looking good for Crew Finch!

But, do you know what? Wherever Crew Finch appear on the year group league table, I do not doubt the effort they have all been putting in, both in Crew and in classes. The data tells me all I need to know and I'm super proud of them all 😊

The HoWLs of her whole Crew have improved significantly through reflection, pledges and holding each other to account. This has resulted in a significant improvement in their academic progress.

Attendance

Second only to ensuring our students are safe, attendance is the most important function of our school. If our students aren't here, we can't affect them can we?

I feel it is a mistake to think that attendance is a jigsaw piece. That to improve attendance, you just focus on physically getting kids into your school. I have heard conversations with colleagues about process, strategies, tricks and incentives to improve attendance, and they rarely focus on the most important aspect of attendance.

For us to have good attendance, our students need to want to come to school.

This is the most important thing.

Second is that parents support their children to come to school.

There is not much point on working on the wording of a stern attendance letter if these two things aren't in place. Fining parents is even worse. We have never issued a fine to a parent for non-attendance of their children. This is the opposite of what we should be doing.

The importance list for attendance is:

1   Do our children want to come to our school?
2   Do our parents support our children coming to our school?
3
4   Clarity of message
5   Accountability processes

If you are a colleague who is working tirelessly on improving attendance, and you feel you have exhausted all avenues, and your attendance has 'plateaued', and it's still really low, I suggest you step back, take a breath, then imagine you are a student of your school. Ask yourself, *'would I want to come to my school?'.*

If you imagine barriers or reasons why you would not, maybe write them down. Maybe you can start with these things?

Maybe your list might look like this:

- Do I feel safe? Do I feel I have a voice?
- Am I worried about something? Who could I go to, to help?
- Do I enjoy my time at school? Do I know the purpose?
- Do I like my environment? Am I treated kindly?

A lot of the things we do at XP addresses these issues:

- We are a human-scale school. We know our students and our students know us.
- We have Crew for 45 minutes every morning.
- Our curriculum is engaging, immersive, experiential and we create authentic products that enhance the world around us.
- We celebrate our students and our student work.
- We treat our students with compassion and respect.

When we know a student doesn't want to come to school, we work damned hard to sort the issues, which may be extremely complicated.

And this is the key to our high attendance. We do not believe blanket policies and processes work. Each student has different reasons for poor attendance. Sometimes it's that they were genuinely ill, or they had a bereavement in the family, or there is a situation in the family that is outside our control.

We know and record each student's reason and consider if we can do something about it, or not. If we cannot, then we do not waste our time or resources. It is how it is, and we get on.

If we cannot do anything about it, we ensure that we do not send letters home, or constantly hold them to task on their poor attendance. We just promote the positive message that every day at school matters.

If a student's poor attendance is something that we can work on, we start with a conversation involving the student's parents or carers to get to the bottom of things. These conversations can be difficult and sometimes embarrassing for parents, who maybe have just taken their kid on a cheap holiday.

Our parents know that they will have a challenging conversation with their Crew leader, not an anonymous £60 fine for a holiday that was £500 cheaper anyway.

As a parent, I have had attendance letters for my son, who was genuinely ill, and it just made me feel that a) the school doesn't know us well, and b) they have wasted resources sending the letter, as it just got screwed up and thrown in the bin.

Sending fines and inappropriate letters is the opposite of creating strong relationships with parents and understanding why their child isn't attending school as much as they should be.

Our rule of 'no alarms and no surprises' when it comes to communication with parents comes into play here. No letter is sent unless a Crew leader has already contacted the parent, and all letters sent are agreed with the Crew leader.

We then have an attendance intervention process that monitors closely, with weekly parental check ins, the improvement.

We have a weekly 'attendance league' to encourage positive peer pressure and Crew competition, celebrating this success, and comparing ourselves against local and national averages. The number of 'late marks' is like the goal difference of a football league.

Our attendance ladder and Crew attendance mountain visualises our success in Crew, and importantly equates the percentage attendance to days and weeks off school over the year. 90% attendance means 20 days, or 4 whole weeks off school.

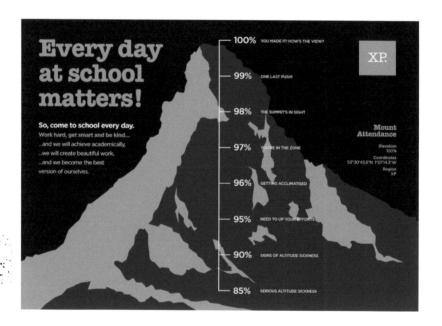

Our student attendance is between 96-97%.

2017 data shows the average attendance in Doncaster is 93%, and nationally it is 94.6%.

Promoting good behaviours

I recently visited a local school to try and kickstart the process of sharing best practice locally. One of the outcomes of my visit was an understanding that while both schools take very different approaches to many things, we ultimately want to achieve many similar outcomes.

This reminded me of an anecdote I heard about the american political Kennedy family. When a younger sibling asked his dad how he could be in a room with 'those Republicans' and talk civilly with them, when he hated them so much, his dad replied, *'son, we all want what's best for America, we just have different ideas on how to achieve it'*. I use this to remind me to be civil even when my head is screaming. Our colleagues work extremely hard to do what they think is right, even if don't agree with how they do it. We need to hold onto that, while being able to express our own ideas passionately and persuasively. I'm still learning...

A great moment of clarity came to me when we consider behaviour in the classroom. All schools, no matter what the context and approach, want our students to have good behaviours in their classroom.

During my visit, one of the key observations was the consistent teacher walls. They had the projected screen displaying the learning targets of the lesson and stretch goals. Next to the screen there was the 'consequences board'. This was consistent in every classroom.

The consequences board allows teachers to write the names of the students showing poor behaviours, and to tick off C1 to C4, so the students can see their poor behaviours being noted, counting their chances until they were removed from the class.

Consequences Board				
Name	C1	C2	C3	C4

It is a perfectly clear example of reactively punishing poor behaviours.

In our school, we have consistent teacher walls too. We also display our learning targets, but next to our screens are our character traits, our habits of work and learning, then three wipe boards titled, 'working hard', 'getting smart' and 'being kind'. On these boards, our teachers write the names of the students displaying these characteristics.

This is a perfectly clear example of promoting good behaviours.

This continues through our Crew and community meetings where students and staff appreciate good behaviours of others, are allowed to make stands for character values if they feel others aren't showing them, and are able to apologise to their peers if they made mistakes.

Where a student has made a mistake that needs to be sorted before they can join the community again, they are given time to reflect on their behaviours and suggest how they can put things right.

Reflection

When we have to remove a student from their community, we give them time and guidance to reflect on their behaviours, take ownership of what they could have done differently, suggest how they can put things right and pledge to react differently.

This may include apology; both personal and public, or some kind of community service. Again, Crew is where the checks and balances take place. Is the reflection authentic and appropriate? Have they stuck to their pledges?

Exclusion

While reflection works as a short (one morning session) intervention, sometimes an internal exclusion is appropriate for respite and to show others that certain behaviours are not acceptable at all. We recognise that most of the time, the student is best being at school, rather than being sent home.

However, we do sometimes fixed-term exclude a student from school, again for respite and to reinforce that some behaviours are not acceptable.

We do not believe any student should be permanently excluded. This doesn't make sense to us. Our official statement is:

"If all stakeholders act collegiately and collaboratively, then we do not believe any student should be permanently excluded".

We do recognise that this is a big 'IF', and it includes local schools and the Local Authority.

It means that we will exhaust all avenues, and we sometimes forge new roads if we have to. Habits and attitudes are hard to break when formed against the local context of high exclusion rates. We ask that schools, like children, should be treated equitably, but that is hard for process and adults who believe that equality is the right way.

I like the phrase, 'whatever it takes', from Ed Vainker's Reach Academy and I look forward to learning what that looks like when I visit them. I'm aware they are a different school to XP in a number of ways, but I have read many admirable things that they do, and that we should.

We are not the only school in Doncaster that takes this approach. In fact, Andy's old school, Campsmount under the leadership of the new Headteacher, Adam Dale, is even going one step further and trying not to even fixed-term exclude any student. I will be extremely proud of Adam when his exclusions are lower than us. Because we do lots of things differently, we aren't a fair comparison for other schools with high exclusions, but Campsmount are. They are the inconvenient truth, not us.

A last word on permanent exclusion in the UK...

The Local Authority has a legal responsibility to ensure every child has an education. If the LA doesn't work constructively with you to provide a suitable education for a child, your last resort is to permanently exclude. Then the LA must provide an education for that child. So permanent exclusion doesn't make sense on any level. I'm not saying it's easy though. I heard the other day that 85% of people in our prisons were permanently excluded from school. It's hard, complex and very important work not to do this.

High exclusions create an underclass in our towns and cities, and I don't want this for my hometown of Doncaster.

To wrap up the chapter on behaviour, I'd like to share a couple of pointers from my giants, Ron Berger (EL) and Larry Rosenstock (HTH).

Ron talks about EL students having a sense of purpose *'beyond themselves'*, that they are part of something bigger than their individuality. We see this moral imperative or noble mission in our better Expeditions, such as 'spread a little happiness', where our students spend time with elderly people and make beautifully crafted boxes full of gifts that relate to their lives, alongside a biography of what our students have learnt from them and an essay response to the guiding question, 'can kindness change the world'.

We also see this when our students form study groups to get each other through the standards test. Even though the whole education system focuses on individual success, they are not on their own. They are Crew.

When I challenged Larry on how their students are so eloquent even though there are no design principles or explicit teaching of character at HTH, he simply replied, *"well... we treat them with respect for a start...!"*

I love how HTH has such implicit beauty.

I think that is, pretty much, the start and the end.

Nothing is more important than Crew

On the first day of school at XP and XP East, students get on a bus and go on an Outward Bound experience. Often students have never met each other, except briefly on our Transition Day, and sometimes they are the only student from their primary school. Students sleep in the woods, climb a mountain and work together through this physically and emotionally challenging situation to answer the guiding question, 'What is Crew?' When they depart for the experience they are a group of individuals, when they return they are Crew.

So what is Crew?

Crew takes place every morning for forty five minutes students. It is a group of twelve to thirteen students who are led by a Crew Leader. This group of often disparate and different students circle up together to reflect on the Habits of Work and Learning, our Character Traits and are allowed to develop their individuality through using their voice and finding who they are.. We get to know each other in Crew and this becomes the central support mechanism for students in school. Crew is where we hold each other to account is something isn't going well either in terms of academic progress or behaviour.

Crew offers a safe place where students can be themselves and ask either implicitly or explicitly for help and guidance from their peers. From simple check-ins to sharing stories about their lives, Crew offers students a place where they can be who they are and allows them to grow into the best versions of themselves. Through these intimate and sometimes brutally honest interactions students grow their characters in a way I have never witnessed in any educational setting. In most secondary schools students might have Tutor Time, (I know from bitter experience) where a register is taken, students sit on the desks with their coats on, have a homework planner signed, if they've remembered to bring it, and then they are 'dismissed' to start their day. What a missed opportunity.

In Crew, students share who they are outside of school, what makes them tick and what makes them stop. For example, on a Monday students check-in and then share what they have been doing over the weekend or over the holidays. A simple waste of time, right, when they could be focusing on extra English or Maths?

Wrong.

This is time well spent on developing a unique bond between each other in Crew that will be invaluable when stuff doesn't go to plan.

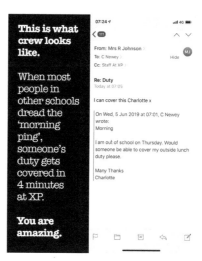

This is what crew looks like.

When most people in other schools dread the 'morning ping', someone's duty gets covered in 4 minutes at XP.

You are amazing.

Often students make mistakes. Students reflect on these mistakes and make pledges about how they are going to put them right. Who holds the students to account for these pledges.

Crew.

And why? Because they trust their Crew and their Crew Leader. Because they have developed strong bonds starting with the Outward Bound experience and continuing with the mountain we all climb called school.

Crew activities include: Check-ins; reflections; academic support and mentoring; reading independently; study groups; focusing on and discussing our HoWLs; making academic and character pledges; team building and problem solving; preparing for Student Led Conferences; focusing on topical issues... To name just a few. And these all contribute to the academic and character growth of students.

In Crew we learn how to get smart.
In Crew we learn the purpose, meaning and reward of working hard.
In Crew we learn to be kind to each other.

As the students say, 'Crew is our family.'

Nothing is more important than Crew.

Appreciations, Apologies, Pledges and Stands

Every Friday morning the whole school meets together in our central space and we hold a Community Meeting. This is not an assembly - far from it - this is a chance for us to come together as a whole community and reflect on the week we have had and what the following week will look like. After a short reading or a focus on Character Traits or HoWLs the students take over.

During this time, students and staff will openly appreciate others for helping and supporting them in school. It is absolutely mind blowing to listen to students do this publicly and without fear nor favour. Students will appreciate staff for organising fieldwork, friends for helping them through rough patches, Crew for holding them to account, classmates for helping them academically. It's mad and at times unbelievable. But it creates a very powerful culture of celebration.

Students also use this time to openly apologise if they have made mistakes. For example, they might have been disrespectful to a member of staff or have shown unkindness towards another student. This allows them to put it right but to do it in front of everyone so that there is a collective reassurance that our culture is being protected. But it doesn't stop there. Apologies can just be words so we expect a pledge from the student about how they will put right the mistake. Often, students have reflected deeply about what they have done wrong and the pledges they need to commit to to put this right.

The critical point is that students don't pledge 'to not do it again' but come up with concrete ways they are actively going to be more respectful of staff or kinder to their peers. This level of reflection and positive action is highly effective in students developing positive behaviours and understanding social agency.

Another feature of Community Meetings is to allow all students a voice. They use this in a highly effective way by 'making stands' that are linked to our Character Traits and HoWLs. For example, last year a Year 8 student 'Made a Stand' for 'Respect' by asking other students if they would show more mindfulness by flushing the toilets after use as they were often left in a bit of a state!

Can you imagine this? I didn't have to berate students for not looking after facilities at XP. They do it themselves and it has more resonance and efficacy.

Sometimes, through 'Stands' and issue will arise like the wearing of jewelry or the use of mobile phones. So we will set up a working group, during Crew, of interested students to consider the issue and report back to the next Community Meeting with proposals. This empowers all students and is solution driven. As a result stewardship is strong at XP. Students own their school so they look after it and there have been countless examples of where this has been a focus in 'Stands'.

Community meetings allow us to reflect deeply on culture.

Community meetings allow us to be openly kind to one another and hold each other to account.

Community meetings allow us to be a community.

Perhaps the biggest immediate difference to most other schools that people see, is XP's curriculum, or rather, how we deliver the curriculum.

At XP, our curriculum is engaging, purposeful, authentic, visceral and academically rigorous. It is hard work and complicated to put together, and we're extremely proud of the quality of education our students experience. They produce beautiful work, progress academically and become better people.

Our teachers work creatively to collaboratively construct the curriculum, keeping our staff interested, invested and invigorated.

To accomplish this, our teachers also design their timetable. They teach what they want, when they want, within the constraints of a working school with limited resources.

It is focused on doing more than just getting good grades for our students, but not at the expense of this. By creating a high quality curriculum, you can achieve more, and this takes time and resources, and is seen as an investment, much like good parenting, or good design.

Our curriculum is knowledge-rich, standards-based, teacher-led, and allows our students to express who they are through their work. Our students work really hard because they enjoy the work. Just like we as adults do. Our curriculum is also experience-rich, utilising the community that surrounds us to provide experts that are often only too happy to share their passion with our students and staff. Our children experience more than just the four walls of their classroom.

Powerful knowledge

While some schools espouse the concept of 'Knowledge Is Power', knowledge in and of itself is not powerful. It's what you do with that knowledge that starts to make it powerful. KIP schools tend to focus on standards-based exam results to show that they are enhancing our children's life chances. But that isn't the whole, or indeed, the end of the story.

In an age where knowledge is abundant and largely freely available, the concept of 'Cultural capital' builds on this to give context to knowledge to leverage its power. While this is great, the greater aspect of knowledge, to make it truly powerful is to empower our children to act and impact positively on the world around them. When we construct our curriculum, we ask ourselves, what is the powerful knowledge we need to give to our students to act? To make an impact on the world around them?

Powerful Knowledge is what our curriculum is built on...

Cultural capital allows us to see our place in the world. Powerful knowledge[11] enables us to affect the world we live in. If cultural capital enables social mobility, then powerful knowledge enables social equity.

There's one thing knowing that there's something called a university[12]. There's another thing visiting the university to see that you could be part of it. There's another thing entirely doing purposeful work at the university with experts and professional equipment to bring the data back to the classroom. Not just knowing about science, or doing some science, but being a scientist.

This Powerful Knowledge in XP's curriculum was evident in the Expedition, *"From the ground up"*, where the students were asked the question, *"What does the community of Doncaster owe to the miners?"*.

They didn't just learn that there are coal seams under Doncaster, or why they were formed. They interviewed and wrote biographies of miners, pit nurses and people who grew up through the miners strike. They didn't just visit the headquarters of the National Union of Miners, but they went there when the enquiry about Orgreave was cancelled, and they were interviewed by the Guardian newspaper. The students' opinions were published in a national newspaper.

That is Powerful Knowledge.

Dr Richard Pountney

"Cultural capital is where an individual is defined by his or her embodied (skills and attributes), objectified (belongings), and institutionalised (education and skills) assets in addition to their economic wealth and social class. It is having assets that give social mobility.

Cultural capital is something given to you or that you gain, regardless of whether you are entitled to it or whether it is socially just for you to have it. Cultural capital is something you have that others might not. The word 'capital' suggests it operates in a market and is subject to competition. A meritocracy.

Powerful Knowledge is where learners have been given fair access to expertise and a fair distribution of knowledge that prepares them to be successful in the modern world. This is epistemic justice, and it goes beyond simplistic notions of learners' employability (the right to work) in order to uphold learners' access to powerful knowledge (the right to think) as a form of social justice, in which young people can be given access to new contexts – and to understand not just how the world can be different, but how their place in the world can be different and how they might positively impact on that world.

Powerful Knowledge is something that all should be given access to. It is more than the material worth of something – it is the symbolic advantage of having understanding of something in order that this can be applied for the good of oneself and of one's community.

A democracy."

11 Pountney, R. and McPhail G. (2019) Crossing boundaries: exploring the theory, practice and possibility of a 'Future 3' curriculum, British Educational Research Journal, DOI 10.1002/berj.3508

12 Pountney, R. and Said, M. (2018) Developing effective learners through a school/university partnership in curriculum making. Impact 3. [online: https://bit.ly/2LmXn8q]

A quick timetable overview

Rather than delivering curriculum standards through the conventional discrete lesson chunk, XP runs 'Learning Expeditions'. Generally, they are term long (8 weeks) and split into Humanities & Arts (HUMAN) and Science, Technology, Engineering, Arts & Mathematics (STEAM). But this is flexible, and we've done Expeditions that are two terms and cross both humanities and sciences.

Alongside this, we run Spanish conventionally in discrete lessons, and every week, we have sessions called X-Block (short for exploratory, and borrowed from HTH) where we run sessions on subjects that may not fit into the Expedition, such as music, drama, computer science, PE etc.

We have Crew (our pastoral system) for 45 minutes every morning and community meetings every week (whole school and year groups).

We have intervention sessions called JOLT (Jump On Learning Targets) where students can respond to marking, and JOLT+ which are sessions that teachers can focus on specific interventions to support and challenge our students.

From Year 9, we have Duke of Edinburgh Award (DofE) sessions where our students complete Bronze and Silver DofE awards.

We cover the National Curriculum standards from Year 7 and GCSE Core subject standards from at least Year 9. Our 'Core' GCSEs are the subjects we map standards to Expeditions, which all our students do. These are Maths, English Language, English Literature, Science (Which counts for two GCSEs), History, Art and Spanish.

Every Wednesday afternoon, from Year 9, our students partake in 'Common Mission'. These sessions focus on personalised activities that are designed to allow our students to explore their own interests and career pathways. Most choose to study an extra qualification such as Business, Computer Science, Engineering, Drama, Music, Geography, Citizenship, Health and Fitness, whereas others follow their passion without a qualification, for instance, they use their time to set up a social enterprise instead of doing Business GCSE, access provision at the Northern Racing College or focus on additional study of their core subjects.

The students not completing a qualification are expected to create a high quality portfolio of work that proves to others what they can do.

Our classes are heterogeneous, mixed-ability groupings of 25 students in two classes per year group, until our Expeditions finish at Christmas in Year 11. At this point, our students form 'study groups' for each subject. Some simply stay together for each subject, for instance History and English, whereas others form smaller groups as the curriculum is split into 'Foundation and 'Higher' curriculums for Maths, Spanish and Science.

Post 16, our students study through subject-deep Learning Expeditions, purposeful professional internships, and personal projects that will allow them to access their next destination.

Narrative is extremely important in our curriculum. We create the story of the Expedition first, we weave in history, the Expedition text and careers interactions. Our study of the arts allow us to appreciate the world around us and add to the world's narrative.

The anatomy of a Learning Expedition

While each Learning Expedition can be different, there are elements that are usually consistently present:

- The title (usually a reference to a punk song...[13])
- The guiding question
- The long-term learning targets (referring to the NC or GCSE standards)
- The text - normally a book, but could be a film, a website etc
- The immersion event
- The case studies
- Fieldwork / experts / service learning
- The product(s) that students will create.
- The significant assessment pieces
- The culmination (The presentation of learning, or other event)
- The curation and legacy left by the Expedition

---

[13] *"I fought the law, and the law won"*, was a good one. My favourite so far though isn't a song. It is for a history Expedition. The kids had to learn about the Normans for their GCSE, so the teachers called it, *"Norman Wisdom"*. It was funny because the kids didn't know why it was funny.

THE ANATOMY OF A LEARNING EXPEDITION

IMMERSION / HOOKS / KICK OFF
(VISCERAL EXPERIENCE)

GUIDING QUESTION

PURPOSE

| CASE STUDIES 1 | CASE STUDIES 2 | CASE STUDIES 3 |

TEXT

FIELDWORK ASSESSMENTS
PORTFOLIO EXPERTS
ARTEFACTS OF LEARNING

PRODUCT
(SOMETHING THE KIDS CREATE)

EXHIBITION
(CELEBRATION/PRESENTATION OF LEARNING)

MAKE IT PUBLIC!!

CURRICULUM MAPPING → ENERGY

STANDARDS-BASED
KNOWLEDGE-RICH
TEACHER-LED

→ HIGH — BOOKS
— VIDEOS
→ LOW — EVENTS
— SPEECHES
— CoL

PROJECT MANAGEMENT

JEFF'S LAW
↓

TOBY'S LAW
↓

PLANNING
- ONE LEADER (COMMUNICATION)
  - NARRATIVE
  - OVERVIEW
  - FIRST WEEK PLANNED

'DONE!
- REGULAR CHECK-INS/REVIEW
- ASSESSEMENTS GRADED
- FIX DONE (PURPLE PEN / RED BOX WORK)
- PORTFOLIOS SIGNED OFF
- PRODUCT FINISHED
- EXHIBITION DONE
- EXPEDITION CURATED

→ DO THE PROJECT FIRST!!!

Around this structure is our progress cycle:

- Curriculum content and coverage
- Expedition planning
- Assessment
- Interventions
- Portfolios of evidence
- Tracking of completeness
- Celebrations / Presentations of Learning
- Cross-moderation
- Expedition review

Our Expeditions allow us to:

- Teach kids stuff so they pass their exams
- Give them visceral experiences of the world
- Put our students outside their comfort zones so they grow as people
- Give them opportunities for social activism, i.e. Make the world a better place
- Hold their interest
- Give them a sense of purpose ie Why am I here? Why am I doing this?
- Engage their head, heart and hands for a wider education
- Bring parents / significant others into the experience
- Bring the community into the school and the school into the community
- Create narratives of learning that we can build on in the future
- Give opportunities for individual and team work, problem solving and all the other stuff businesses say they want from education
- Give our students a sense of purpose beyond themselves as individuals

I think I could go on forever listing the reasons why we do Expeditions, rather than discrete, subject-based lessons. It does take a lot more effort to deliver, but what you get out far outweighs what you put in, and it is good work, so you have more energy to do it.

Apart from the top point, the rest of the reasons for doing Expeditions is the opposite of what you do when you just teach discrete, subject-based lessons.

If you want to ask, why do all this, when it is much cheaper and more simple to get kids good academic outcomes by just teaching them stuff, and all the rest is a distraction, I would say that qualifications open doors, and it is who you are, and the quality of the work that you produce that will get you the job, place at university, or startup business loan. Which is why we do more.

I would also look at the children that schools that focus just on academic outcomes are failing, and it tends to be those children who don't conform, who are low ability, low income, or with special educational needs.

I would be one of those children who wouldn't conform. I would have got into trouble and not got to university. I don't know what my life would have been like if that had happened to me as a child. Knowing the issues I was facing as a child, I probably wouldn't be here right now.

Learning Expeditions work for the vast majority of children, including the highest ability as there is no ceiling to the quality of work you can produce. Some of our student work is of such high quality, it is indistinguishable from that of an adult professional.

Examples of Learning Expeditions

The best way to see examples of our Expeditions is through our digital curation. Please go to: **www.xpschool.org/curriculum**

If you just have our book, the next few pages contain narratives of just a few of the Expeditions that we have done.

Unapologetic Expeditionists

Expeditions - at the heart of creativity and curriculum at XP – are always led by a guiding question. So from *'When is it Right to Rebel?'* to *'What does our Community owe to the Railways?'*, this question is always referred back to as an Expedition progresses, through immersion, research and finally with the creation of a product.

Products are as diverse as books, posters, events – such as a poetry slam, exhibitions and art installations. They are always designed to be part of the community, making a positive impact on local people and places, and vitally, part of the real world.

Recent Expeditions from XP students resulted in the publication of two books. The first, based on the mining history of Doncaster (*'From The Ground Up - What does our Community owe to the Miners'*), rapidly became a best seller in the local history genre. It was closely followed by a companion book (*'Society, Steam and Speed - What does our Community owe to the Railways'*) which outsold the first one. Both books were sold online and in Waterstones.

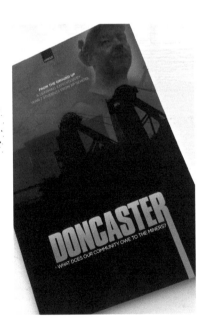

'When is it Right to Rebel?' was a timely guiding question that coincided with the centenary of Women's Suffrage in the UK. Suffragette sashes were made by all 50 students engaged with this Expedition – each choosing a cause or idea they would champion.

The sashes were displayed at the heart of the Frenchgate Centre in Doncaster – a stunning centrepiece, viewed over several weeks by hundreds of thousands of visitors.

Similarly, the *'Don't Mention the War'* exhibition - with the guiding question *'What Should we Remember?'* was an exploration of the interpretation of war through the lives of notable figures, but also those known only to their families and friends, who gave their lives or lived through the visceral experience.

This exhibition at the Doncaster Museum and Art Gallery also became part of the 1914 -1918 digital archive.

Legacy, as well as continuous engagement with our community, is also important to us. So, highlights such as the donation of student art – in this case a screenprint – to our historic Mansion House as part of a town-wide print trail, underlines for us the power of beautiful work. It's part of what gives our work, our Expeditions, our products, purpose and life.

Melanie Hewitt I Community Engagement Officer I XP Trust

Creating a Learning Expedition

At XP, we say our Expeditions start with the standards, as opposed to pure PBL which starts with the project idea, but in reality it's a bit like writing a pop song; sometimes the lyrics come first, sometimes the tune, but most of the time, they bounce off each other and influence each other through the creative process.

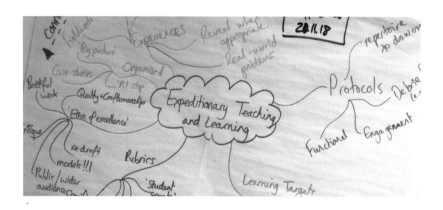

Anyway, officially our Expeditions start with the standards, and we use four things to help us shape our Expeditions and therefore our curriculum:

Standards Maps – this is a list of the standards that we need to cover and include the National Curriculum Standards, and GCSE standards. They show which year we cover them (using the progress maps as a guide), and which Expeditions we cover them in (using the curriculum maps as a guide). They show which year we cover them (using the progress maps as a guide), and which Expeditions (using the curriculum maps as a guide).

Curriculum Maps – these are like big jigsaw puzzles that show the big picture of what we cover and where.

Progress Maps – this lists what order we cover the standards, in terms of school years.

Equity of Opportunity – this is a list of things we want all our students to have experienced, like purposeful work at a university, creating a book etc.

In the UK at least, these dynamic documents are key to:

1 Prove that you cover the curriculum, and therefore exist as a school.

2 Keep track of what you have and haven't covered so the kids do well in their exams.

Our teachers get together as Year teams. This can be as little as two teachers (one for each class), up to four teachers that give input into Maths, English, HUMAN and STEAM. At Key Stage 4, we have inputs from Maths, English, Science, History, Art and Spanish. Post 16, our students do subject deep Expeditions.

The Year teams, with input from the subject leads, map out the curriculum for their particular Year. They have access to all the curriculum from previous years, so this is a blend of old and new, depending on what the teachers want to do.

For each Expedition, before they can start it, they have to complete the tasks defined by Jeff's Law.

Jeff's Law

The purpose of Jeff's Law is to ensure the minimum requirements for starting a Learning Expedition have been completed and shared. These are:

A leader has been assigned

The Expedition leader is the communications conduit within their team and out to the wider staff. The leader is expected to know, or be able to find out, the state of the Expedition and be able to communicate any issues, or needs, or celebrations. The leader is not expected to do everything in the team, but they are expected to ensure effective delegation of process.

A narrative has been created

This is the story of the Expedition and is written in past tense, to aid both a sense of completion and for the curation of the Expedition. A template and example narrative are available.

Daily schedule

This is the overview of the Expedition, with a short day by day plan. An example and template are available.

Done the project first

This means that the teacher has created a model of the work to be done by students. Each element should be modeled and/or exemplified. This is shared publicly with all staff. This model does not have to be shared with the students if the teacher has a good reason not to.

At least the first week of detailed planning completed

Using the template planning documents, teachers are expected to have planned the lessons for their first week of teaching in detail, including the daily learning targets, activities and assessments in each lesson. These milestones must be seen by two school leaders. The leaders will sign to say they have seen all these elements with their own eyes and know how to access them in the future.

Once this has been signed off, the lead teacher gets a certificate!

The reason we do this, is because this is the minimum planning you should do to ensure a successful Expedition. Otherwise teachers tended to drift towards the easiest flow of the day, which is to turn up and teach kids stuff. Our teachers are really good, so this is the worse case scenario; our kids get taught by good teachers. But we want more at XP, so unless Jeff's Law is completed, the Expedition doesn't start. You might as well just teach kids stuff.

It's been close a few times, but we've never yet had an Expedition not start on time. Thanks to Jeff and his law...!

Assessment of learning in Expeditions

We use assessments 'of' and assessment 'for' learning throughout a Learning Expedition. Our process is detailed in our assessment handbook, but to summarise, we identify assessment opportunities during the Expedition.

Assessments of learning are used to determine whether a student has met a learning target. Students will always have at least two assessments of learning for each learning target. These assessments could include formats such as; a test, a presentation, an experiment, a speech or a piece of writing, for example. Students will be given an assessment rubric which describes how their work will be graded and the qualities in the work required for success. This rubric will link to the long-term and supporting learning targets for each Expedition.

We will use our professional judgement to determine the final grade for a particular learning target rather than taking an average of the assessments of learning for that target. This means we can give credit for improved performance and progress over time. Furthermore, one piece of work might be used as an assessment of learning for more than one learning target and this will be reflected in the assessment rubric for that piece of work.

Our principles regarding assessment are:

- We will involve students in the grading process.
- We will use only individual work for grades.
- We will give students at least two chances to meet a learning target in an assessment of learning.
- We will use our professional judgement to determine the grade for a particular learning target, giving credit for improved performance over time.
- We will not include an N (0) grade in any average for an overall Expedition grade. The student must complete the work.
- We will report on academic targets and HoWL targets separately.
- We will provide clear rubrics or success criteria for every piece of work that will be graded.

- We will measure the standard of each piece of work on its own merit, rather than in comparison with the work of others.
- We will align our assessment criteria with national standards to ensure at least expected progress.
- We may revise target grades upwards where students continue to exceed their target.
- We will never revise target grades downwards.
- We will use assessments to motivate and prepare our students to be 'university ready'.

Fixing work

Any work that is below the minimum expected grade (MEG) of the student is expected to be FIXed. It stood for 'Formal Interventions at XP', but we just adopted it into our language and students naturally talk about fixing their work. They are given support and challenge to do this. This is normally done outside lesson time.

We are trying to put more energy into HoWLs interventions that academic ones, as detailed in the behaviour section, as it is much more effective.

Student portfolios

While a lot of the student work is naturally digital in nature, we value our physical student portfolios, which are proudly displayed for all to see and access in the library section of our school. For each Expedition, the portfolio starts with the Expedition contents page which details all the artefacts the students have completed, cross-referenced to the learning targets which relate to NC (National Curriculum) and GCSE standards. This explicitly shows how students have met the targets and to what level, compared with their starting positions.

While it is best practice to finish off all work, and neatly bring everything together, it is also the perfect way to prove to outside stakeholders that our cross-subject Learning Expeditions are academically rigorous and to show progress explicitly.

I'm sure our student portfolios nailed our Ofsted 'outstanding' judgement. They should have done. They are stunning.

I'm sure that in the very near future, our students will have a complementary digital portfolio, but while we are embedding our practice, there is something existentially important about being able to physically pick up any student's portfolio, and know it is still there in the library when you leave the school. When we get this practice consistently right, we can move on to digital portfolios.

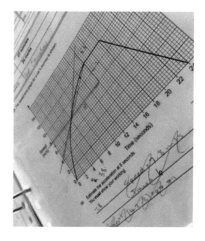

Toby's Law

The word, 'done' at XP is a sacred word! Like we use Jeff's Law to ensure we start an Expedition the right way, Toby's Law enables us to finish each Expedition the right way, by getting it done.

When we were culminating our very first Expedition, *"What makes a successful community?"*, during the book launch, we discovered that one of our student's pages had not been included, despite hours of proof-reading. The student was called Toby Williamson. We were absolutely devastated. Much more so than Toby! To get round this, we created a cover sleeve for the book and included Toby's work and the law that we would never get this wrong again.

We've adapted this notion to check systematically that we have:

• Graded all the key summative assessments, with FIX completed.

• Students have finished their final product work

• The work has been made public through an exhibition

• Student portfolios are complete

• The work has been curated physically and / or digitally

• The Expedition has been reviewed with curriculum maps updated

Toby's Law

Inexplicably, despite hours and hours spent proof-reading the final product, not to mention all the hard work by every student not just to get the book done, but all the preparations for the Celebration of Learning, we discovered during the Book Launch that one of our student's pages had not been included.

That student was Toby Williamson. To say we were all devastated would be an understatement. Toby was part of the Book Launch team! How would we fix this? It would cost us thousands to get all the books printed again?

At XP, we learn through experience. The shared narrative of these experiences is an important part of creating memories, not just remembering facts. Instead of hiding our mistake, we decided to make it part of our narrative, so no-one will forget.

We are making a stand for Craftsmanship and Quality, and have pledged never again to allow any product we create to not include all the work by all our students. This will never happen again. This is called, 'Toby's Law'.

Cover illustration

Toby Williamson
Crew : Armstrong

In my opinion, social aspects are by far the most important factors in any successful community. I believe this because, no matter how beautiful and self-sustaining a community may be, it won't work if nobody gets along. Social aspects are also vital in creating a sense of community...

Although social aspects are incredibly important in creating and maintaining a successful community, a community won't flourish if it doesn't have a clean and peaceful environment for it to exist in. For this to be a reality, everyone must respect public places...

As well as this, it is important to respect local animals and their habitats as the ecosystem will fail without them...

Nobody can survive on their own, and this is visible throughout the animal kingdom, from the Emperor penguins who huddle together to survive the harsh Arctic winters to meerkats who work together in order to look after their young, hunt for food and keep an eye out for predators. Humans mirror these traits, banding together to get through difficult times as well as contributing towards a functioning community. Everybody needs others. Everybody needs community...

We have a wider team of technicians, administrators and learning coaches to help with all this.

The difference between Learning Expeditions and PBL

First of all, PBL (Project-based learning) is being used as a catch-all phrase in education land, which isn't always helpful.

I want to compare and contrast 'pure' PBL, as extolled by my good friend Jeff Robin, who was a pioneering teacher of art at HTH. He was the guy who told me about Ron Berger when we first visited.

I asked Jeff to visit XP at the backend of our third year, and his legacy is enshrined in 'Jeff's Law'[14] that all our teachers have to meet to progress with their teaching of our Learning Expeditions. He was here for a week, and apart from having some fun, he asked me what I wanted him to do. I asked him to just be himself and disrupt something.

After the first day, he said to me, *"I don't know what you guys are doing, but it isn't PBL"*. At the end of the week, he said, *"I'm sort of getting Expeditions. I'm not sure why you do it that way, but the kids really like being here. I think it's because you're not nasty[15] to them."*

We care about our students, and they know it.

We agreed that a good marketing strapline for recruiting students would be, *"Come to XP. We're not nasty."* It would set us apart from the competition.

If there are just three outcomes for schools, maybe it's:

- Academic progress
- Character growth
- Beautiful work

While some schools focus mainly on academic progress, we would say that we focus on the bottom two, and academic progress is a consequence of this.

For me, pure PBL focuses on creating beautiful, authentic work. Work that happens in the world outside of schools. A pure PBL practitioner would argue that character growth and academic progress is a consequence of creating beautiful, authentic work.

It does. I've seen it at HTH. Their academic outcomes speak for themselves. So do their kids.

Working with Jeff, I absolutely admire the genius of clarity to his work, and the fact that he does what he says we should do. His mantra is:

1 Do the project first

2 Unpack the deliverables

3 Teach the deliverables

4 Make the work public

or...

1 Just do something!

The start is the most important thing. 'Do the project first'. If we are asking our kids to do something, then we must be prepared to do it ourselves. Do not be a hypocrite! For some teachers, this is like breaking the fourth wall. But we do it, and we expect it for all our Expeditions, or the teachers don't get to teach it.

---

14 Jeff is the last person in the world to desire a 'law' surrounding his practice. Which is why it's funny!
15 For the record, this isn't the word that Jeff used (twice!).

Finishing the job is the second most important thing. Jeff told me, *"I get my self-worth from finishing things".* At XP, the word, 'Done' is sacred.

I don't think you could create a pure PBL school in the UK. Well, not a government funded one anyway. For a school to exist, they have to prove they have a broad and balanced curriculum, that this is being 'covered', and that students are progressing academically against the curriculum standards.

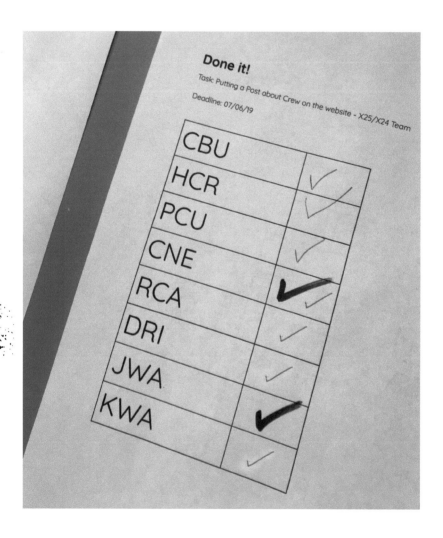

Jeff

What could happen in the UK is create a 'Post Progressive' educational environment. Terry Heick, an American educational philosopher explains, "A progressive education corrects all weaknesses and bolsters deficiencies. A post-progressive education allows minds to bloom and grow and become."

That is what XP tries to do. We care how the students and teachers feel about their learning and teaching and meet everyone where they are and grow from there.

If you are concerned that you did not cover all the standards when in your PBL classroom, that is great. PBL is a way to show the students how and why this subject is used in the real world, it gives context and lets the students feel that the work they are doing is not archaic exercises that everyone has to do.

After the project go back and back fill the standards you missed, the students will have a context for this additional learning and it will be more meaningful. Backfill is good, front load is bad.

Remember...

"ACCOUNTABILITY, n. The mother of caution." Ambrose Bierce

In the UK, teachers just creating projects around their passions would not be enough to prove coverage to our external stakeholders. And some kids learn the hard way, by failing. While I don't have an issue with this, because they do learn eventually, if Ofsted, our school police, saw this being allowed to happen, it would trash your judgement. You would be closed before you got the results that justified your actions.

I'm brave and I'm not risk-averse, but I absolutely know you have to exist to do something. Saying that, I absolutely adore the work of pure PBL and maybe one day, when we agree that assessed portfolios are the way forward, rather than unrigorous, knowledge retrieval exams, and we are granted the freedom, time and space to educate our children properly, maybe then we can move towards pure PBL in the UK.

Careers

When I reflect on being an employer myself, and when I work with other employers, the disjoint between what we do in schools and what employers are looking for, and what students need to be successful in the world outside of school, has never been so stark.

I don't need to talk about what employers want, as they've been saying it consistently for decades. Take a moment to think about what employers say they are looking for, and ask yourself, how does that relate to standards-based tests? How do these tests prepare our children to be successful? I do not know of an employer who will employ you to pass tests for them.

While employers may thank schools for making their HR process slightly easier, they are way more interested in a student's work and their character. Can they do the job? Can I work with them? Students need portfolios to prove they can do the job. They need the best version of themselves to prove they can work with you.

While the education world is lamenting the narrowing of the curriculum, in reference to the creative studies, or languages, it is 'careers' as a subject that has been totally marginalised within schools, reducing it to a few special days when they have a careers fair, or pretend they are the boss of a soap factory, or something equally inane.

Careers in schools in the UK at least is measured in 'interactions', and schools record these to prove they 'do careers'. At least seven quality interactions is good, and has been proven to improve a student's life chances. Hopefully, you can see that in every Expedition we do, we go on purposeful fieldwork, work with experts and produce products that live in the world around us. Each one of these experiences provides a quality interaction with the world outside of school and opens our students' eyes as to the possibilities in work, at university, in life.

As we start to build our Post 16 provision next year, these careers experiences get more and more important and our students need to leave school with much more than grades. Academic progress, beautiful work, character growth.

The work we are currently embarking on is how we can make careers more explicit throughout our whole school, from Year 7 through. It is incredibly important and should be the backbone of all our work to prepare our children to be successful in their next stage of development.

We would not be the school we are today without the technology we use, the way we use it, and importantly, the understanding of why we use it.

Information and communication technology allows us to learn more and learn it faster.

In this chapter, we will not talk about augmented reality, virtual reality, virtual learning environments, the latest app called 'Bizwigglegumpf' that you've not heard of (and hasn't been invented yet), or the amazing training sessions we have for our staff, facilitated by 'Microgoopple' (because we don't do that)

Instead, we will share what has worked for us for the five years of our existence, that has never - touchwood - gone wrong once, and that allows us not to have an IT technician or training for staff.

I'm sure the vast majority of the stuff we use, you will have heard of.

I'm very proud of the way we use technology in XP, especially because my background is in Computer Science and creating educational technology. But maybe I'm proud in a way you might not expect.

The best description I've heard about how we use tech at XP is that it is 'naturally ubiquitous'. We just use it when we need it. It's not a bolt on, or a special lesson, and we don't have a 'computer room'. We just try to use the right tech at the right time for the right reason.

But what is it...?

First off, I want to state that the 'what' of ICT is extremely important to understand the how and why. For me, ICT is a continuum. ICT is anything that allows us to communicate through abstract means.

This is important, because a lot of us see ICT as the latest tech, and not the oldest tech. This blurs and confuses how and why we use it. It creates an importance in how 'innovative' and new things are. It creates a false value in being the first, or having things that others don't.

The killer feature of great technology is that it's easy, fast, simple and it works.

It's easy to see that tech is a continuum by looking at its history. For example, Spotify was an iPod was a Walkman was a record player was a radio was a family standing round a piano having a sing song. Google Docs was Microsoft Word was a word processor was a typewriter was a letter was hieroglyphics was a stone age cave painting.

The point is, is that old tech still works. We have whiteboards that we write on, and take a photo of to share. Our physical student portfolios are visceral, visible and you can't argue with the way they show the academic progress our students make against standards.

If we know what it is, we can make it work for us more effectively. We can use tech to learn more and learn it faster.

There's some kind of curious argument about whether we should use tech in schools, or whether it's just a waste of money. If you see tech as a continuum, like I do, this isn't a question of whether we use tech, but how we use it.

When we use any kind of tech, old or new, we encode our view of the world in order to share it. We could draw a picture of a lion on the whiteboard, and our students would know it was a lion, that it is dangerous, that they live in africa and they eat other animals. Even though it isn't a lion. It's a picture of a lion. An abstract. We use technology to learn more and learn it faster.

We are getting closer to being able to capture reality more and more realistically through virtual and augmented reality, but while this brings our learning experiences closer to reality, it can be quicker, easier, simpler to use abstractions like the written word, or mathematical equations.

Technology is great at showing our children things that are too big, or too small, too expensive or too dangerous to actually experience in real life.

By knowing these things, we can work out what type of tech we should use when learning different things.

Ok, my geek out is now over.

How do we do it at XP?

The set up

We have a fast and reliable internet connection (BT, 1 Gigabit).
We have fast and reliable wifi everywhere in school.

Err... that's it.

We have a server room, but no server in it.

Wait... we have a firewall and filter set to 'not fascist mode but enough to not allow access to the nasty stuff'

Apart from the stuff we need to run the building (CCTV, BMS, phones), that is literally it.

Devices

The devices our staff and students use are not controlled by the school. They are controlled by the people who have them, because they are designed to work like that.

Yes, we allow our students to bring in their own devices. Yes, we sometimes confiscate them when we catch them not using them for educational use. Yes, our kids still talk to each other at dinner and break. Yes, we sometimes have issues with social media spats that get brought into school.

Welcome to 2019.

The vast majority of the time (I will repeat this - the vast majority of time), our staff and students use their devices appropriately and for educational use, doing the amazing things they enable us to do.

We supply our staff with either an Apple laptop (MacBook Air - the best computer ever invented, in my opinion. They will last 7-8 years I reckon, if not 10...), or a ChromeBook (Viglen touchscreen, foldable, robust).

The choice depends on whether staff are creating high quality resources. Mainly our teachers get Apple, and our learning coaches (TAs) get ChromeBooks.

We have a bank of ChromeBooks for kids who don't have their own device for one reason or another (we can supply them through Pupil Premium)

We also have a number of Apple iMacs dotted throughout the school for high quality product work.

Some of our staff (a growing number) have access to iPads with Apple Pencils which are used to explain concepts, producing videos or screenshots.

...I think we have a PC laptop in the cupboard somewhere. We need it to change the answerphone message, apparently. In XP, it is not a M$ world. Soz Bill.

95% of everything we do with devices at XP is using Google Apps (Now called G Suite for Education). They are built from the ground up with collaboration in mind, which is why they work so well. The tools get better all the time. And when I say 'better', I mean faster, simpler, easier. These are our killer features. Fast, simple, easy collaboration.

Training

We don't do training. It is expensive, purposeless and inefficient.

The opposite of training is purpose.

No-one gets trained to use facebook, or their phone. You need to do something, so you grapple with it. If you get stuck, you ask your colleagues or peers or Google. If you are expected to use technology for your work, then that is your purpose, not an excuse for training.

Our training at XP is, *"Here's your laptop, use it..."*

Our diverse staff seem to be using technology extremely well through this approach.

The other saying we have at XP regarding technology is this... *"If we can't use it / understand it / maintain it ourselves, we don't want it."*

We have never had an IT technician. We never will. If we need specialist people to set something up, then we get them in to set it up so we won't have to change anything for a long time.

I've never understood the approach of buying loads of technology then stopping it from working properly. Devices are created now for personalised use (great!), not for Captain Lockdown to assert his control on everything we do (boo!).

While our wifi internet is filtered and logged, most kids have a phone in their pocket with unfiltered internet access. We need to teach them how to use this unbelievable power responsibly, not just assume that kids will do naughty things if we let them.

We have a poster with Spiderman saying, *"WITH GREAT POWER COMES GREAT RESPONSIBILITY"*. This is our IT policy. Use your devices only for educational use when at school, thanks.

Kids can do much more than we think they can, including being responsible and safe. Do they make mistakes? Of course they do, and that's why as adults we put in place appropriate consequences and conversations, so they learn to understand.

Teaching

In each classroom we have a very big TV, 65 inch for most classes, 75 inch in our larger science rooms. They look great and sound great. They are not touch screen. Tactile manipulation is done at device level. You do not have to close the curtains to see them, or reconfigure them every time they get knocked. Their bulbs don't wear out, because they don't have a bulb.

We can cast our device screens to them over wifi, or plug directly into them. They are capable of much more, but we use them for this 99% of the time.

All our planning and resources are created or repurposed using our devices. The vast majority is created in Google Apps, collaboratively. Our curriculum is literacy heavy, and our students still use physical exercise books and portfolio folders, and our teachers print resources, but our curriculum resources are invariably digital.

Our teachers and students also create digital resources that capture specific learning within the classroom. Some teachers capture concepts

How we XP | **Technology**

using an iPad, some simply photograph their whiteboards, or student work. Some learning is captured in the flow of a Google Classroom blog conversation.

The important thing, is that we now put these artefacts somewhere useful. Somewhere more permanent, such as the Expedition Google Site. And this is where we start getting into the 'why'.

In a conventional teaching environment, a classroom, the teacher dictates what learning happens, and when and where it happens. The hope is that students will leave that classroom with more knowledge in their heads than when they came in.

As such, this type of classroom is often referred to as a 'black box'.

We talk about 'exploding the black box' - how can we break the walls down, and allow learning to exist outside these parameters which dictate what, where and when they are learnt?

Teachers should not be the gatekeepers of the curriculum.

Teachers should uncover the curriculum.

Example ▶ Google Sites

We use Google Sites for each of our Learning Expeditions and qualification subjects to tie all our disparate resources together, and present this is an accessible way for our students to not only remember what has been taught, but extend them as well.

This is also a great way to ensure rigour in our teachers' work, as it is public and celebratory.

When we use technology, we ask ourselves how 'APT' is it...? Available, Portable and Transient. Is the learning only available for a certain timescale, e.g in a lesson? Is the learning only available in a certain place, e.g in a classroom? Is the learning available to find, but less so over time?

A shared Google Doc may seem permanent when you create it and share it with someone, but it becomes more transient when you share shed loads of docs with everyone.

You may then add it to a Google Classroom Stream, but again, over time, this will disappear as the blog gets longer.

To make something permanent as we can, we connect it to our school website. This is the one thing that will not go away, and is our starting point for all our digital access. Link from your school website to a Google Site with all your resources, and this is pretty good on the APT scale. It's available any time, any where, and will not move - as long as you have internet access.

We start with a Google Site template that has all the planning resources we need for Expeditions. As we work through them, building the Expedition, we can all see each other's work. Once Jeff's Law is done, we can launch it to our students. As we capture the learning throughout the Expedition, we add it to our website, alongside any extension resources. After the Expedition is finished and Toby's Law is complete, the Expedition is totally curated digitally, ready to share, review, reuse and repurpose.

This allows our curriculum design to fit nicely into the design cycle and achieve continuous improvement.

Example > **Explain Everything** >

A number of our teachers use the app 'explain everything' to capture concepts and record a video is the same time it takes to talk through it.

They use an iPad and Apple Pencil alongside pretty simple resources, such as images and lines and words they draw on the iPad. As the teacher talks through the subject and demonstrates concepts, the app records a video which we then upload to an Expedition Google Site, so our students can access this anytime and anywhere.

Example ⟩ Padlet

Padlet is basically an online, collaborative pinboard, and has been around for ages. It is now so quick and easy to capture WAGOLLs (What A Good One Looks Like - pieces of student work that show a certain great aspect of their learning) and share it with the class. You see a kid's great work, you take a photo of it with your phone – add notes if you want and it's shared with the class. Also good for capturing WASOLLs.

Nothing revolutionary, unless you call things being stupidly easy, fast, simple and working as revolutionary, which we do.

Example ⟩ Google Docs

Pretty much all the design of our school has been done using Google Docs. From policies and process through to our school accounts. Only recently have we moved to an accounts package (Access Education Finance - online & collaborative), and we have built our own MIS (Management Information System) that records attendance and sends our school census to the government.

Google Docs is the single most important reason we have achieved so much in such a short space of time. Online, collaborative technology.

It has allowed us to learn more and learn it faster.

Green Top, the first primary school in the XP Trust, picked it up a couple of years ago. It was like an explosion of productivity.

Of course, I am writing this in a Google Doc.

It has become a meta-technology. I am writing the story about how we have used tech to create our school in the same tech we used...

...anyway, stories are important.

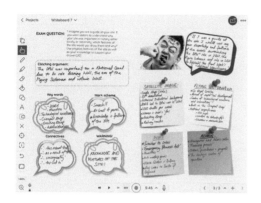

To see more examples of these and the other technologies that we use (realsmart, basecamp etc.) please visit our website:

www.xpschool.org/ howwexp

WE ARE NOTHING...

...BUT STORIES

When I sat in a field in Wales, before we opened XP, I remember realising how important narrative is in schools, and well, life in general. Everything we deem important is captured in stories. When those stories go, we go.

All our Learning Expeditions have a narrative – a story that ties the beginning to the middle to the end – and lets us know where the legacy of the Expedition can be found, whether it is captured digitally on our website, or in a published book in our local Waterstones.

These narratives allow our students to remember the work they have done from Year 7 through to the end of their school years and beyond. When I ask my friends what they can remember about their school days, it almost inevitably will be about an event, or something they made, or a good/bad teacher. Never about a lesson, or knowledge imparted[15].

I can definitely say that I have never heard anyone say, *"That worksheet changed my life"*.

Stories have shaped my life. I didn't have a great upbringing. I had a pretty absent father, and my mother died when I was about 18 months old. When I tell people who have had a stable upbringing, they wonder how I turned out ok, and particularly with this strong sense of a moral compass. I always tell them, it's because I read 2000AD.

2000AD is a British comic, created by Patrick Mills[16] in the 70s. It had everything a six year old boy could wish for. Dinosaurs eating cowboys. A future cop who was 'the law'. Loads of violence and black humour. Bionic stickers for free gifts! I devoured it.

The genius of it though, was that these stories weren't the lame superhero, one man (usually rich, usually upper class) against the evil baddy. They were about capitalism, fascism, feminism and racism. The 'evil' was authority, and our heroes were underdogs, and often working class.

As I grew up, I wasn't scared of authority. I didn't see barriers. If we were right, we could do it. We can win. I believed the stories. I still do.

---

15 I lie. Actually, my great friend Stewart Tavener (PhD Chemist and creator of microphones) said the only thing he could remember from school was from his woodwork teacher. *"Measure twice, Cut once"*

16 One of the proudest moments of my life was when Pat mentioned me in his book, *"Be pure, be vigilant, behave!"*, about the history of 2000AD, and how he hoped his stories would influence his readers. I would be nothing without his stories. Thank you, Pat.

A story about fish and chips

I think it was sometime in 2011 when my wife, Kate and I were working from home and we decided to have a romantic walk through our hometown of Thorne, past the park, to get a bag of chips for lunch from the best chippy in town. The one on the way to the southern train station[17].

As we were walking back, and munching on our chips, I noticed a building with a green roof. I realised it must be 'Green Top' primary school. I'd heard they'd got a new headteacher, and he was pretty good.

At that time, I was struggling with the school our kids, Jac and Dylan were attending. Jac had been looking online for other schools as the behaviour in his class was deteriorating, and I had been told by Dylan's teacher that he was a 'summer child' (he was born 23rd August, so he was the youngest in his year), and that this is seen as an SEN (special educational need), which was why Dylan wasn't progressing academically.

I was born 27th July, and I was ok, so this didn't sit right. I was a governor at the time, and I remember telling Kate that either we find our kids a new school, or I become Chair of Governors and sack the headteacher. I told her which path was the easier to take, but my wife knows best, so our kids were still at the school for now.

Anyway, back to Green Top. I said to my wife, *"Why don't we go and have a look around? If they can't see us now, we can make an appointment"*. So we went in, and luckily the headteacher had a bit of time and showed me around.

Now, when you've visited as many schools as I have, you get this supernatural sense. As soon as you walk into a place, you can sense what they place is like. Some schools feel like they've had the air sucked out of them, and they're horrible. Others feel so welcoming and warm and friendly, and they're ace.

High Tech High overwhelmed me after two hours. Springfield Renaissance in Massachusetts was so overwhelming that I only got down the first corridor to reception, to be faced with the signatures of every single kid for the last five years that had got a place at college.

It was so overwhelming that I had to go straight back out and get some air and look at the sky before I could go back in again. That school was awesome.

Back to Green Top. Neil Butler, the headteacher was chatting to my wife ahead of me, and I was just hanging back, soaking in the atmosphere. It was good. Very good. The area around Green Top wouldn't be described as 'affluent', yet the kids looked happy and were working hard. Funnily enough, my kids' school was rated 'outstanding' and Green Top was rated 'requires improvement'. Hmm... the other way round, me thinks. By the first corner we walked around, I had seen enough. My kids were coming here. When we stopped in the classroom that Dylan would have been joining, the kids' books were out on the table. I picked one up, then another. Then I ushered Kate over. I asked her to picture the work that Dylan was doing, then look in the books in front of her. The work in the books was stunning.

It took me another six months to convince Kate that I knew something about education, and eventually Jac and Dylan joined Green Top (along with a number of other children from the old school!), and they have never looked back. Summer child, my arse. Thank you, Neil and Green Top, for instilling a love of learning in my children. This is the most important gift you could give to any child.

Why am I telling you this mundane story about us moving our kids from one school to another? Well, a couple of years later, Ron Berger visited us from the US and I thought I'd take him round to Green Top. When Ron was about to leave, we were all standing in reception and Ron said, *"So Neil, you're gonna head up the primary division of XP then, right?"*

This was a bit embarrassing because everyone heard, and Neil had to avoid the question. In 2017, Green Top joined the newly formed XP School Trust. In 2019, Neil was named the Primary Executive Principal for the Trust, and he now looks after four schools for us. I am very proud of him.

And thank you Ron, for once again showing me my future.

---

17 It has now changed hands, and the best chippy in Thorne is now the Old Mill chippy, which is more convenient as it's just round the corner from our house. Every time I go in there, they tell me how their son is doing at school and that I must ensure he gets into XP. Fingers crossed, or I'll have to find a different chippy.

Gwyn's story

I was born in Doncaster Royal Infirmary on the 27th July 1971 and I lived in a bungalow with a big garden down Alendale Road, Sprotbrough, Doncaster. I grew up with my dad and sister. My mum had died when I was about 18 months old. She had drowned in the River Don. I went to nursery at Richmond Hill School.

I remember the first day because everyone was crying and I didn't know why. When a nice lady came to me and asked me why I was crying I said, "because everybody else is", then I stopped crying.

I moved schools to Kirkby Avenue in Bentley because my dad had remarried and my step-mum worked there as an English teacher. I remember drinking milk every day and running around the playground pretending I was a superhero with bionic stickers on my arm. I was good at reading and the times tables.

When I moved up to the middle school there, I was allowed to put up my history of soldiers from a comic I was reading called 'Tornado'.

The series ended with a 'future soldier'. These posters stretched all around the ceiling. Tornado eventually merged into the seminal comic, 2000AD which I still read now.

We moved as a family to Sykehouse so me and my sister then went to Stainforth Middle School. I had no friends, so I tried to get a game of footy. I remember lining up and being picked last, and even then reluctantly. I remember doing a move that I learnt from Roy of the Rovers, which I now know as a 'Cruyff turn' and scored. I never got picked last again.

It was at Stainy Middle that I started to realise I wasn't the same as most of my mates. I felt kind of out of step. One day, the school got a BBC Microcomputer, and my life changed. I remember playing a simple Space Invaders game, and a teacher I didn't recognise came in and told me off. He told me that computers were for learning how to program, not play games. When I told him I had programmed it, he didn't believe me so he told me to explain it line by line, so I did. He just walked off, bemused.

When I moved up to Hatfield High School, I didn't see most of my friends again much. I was in Set 1 for everything except French and most of my friends weren't in Set 1 (I deliberately flunked my french test because if you were in Set 1, you did French and German and missed out on PE. I loved PE). I remember being really bored in History and Environmental Science, but Economics was ace, because we had Mr Parkinson, and he was a right laugh. He swore and made jokes and taught us about communism.

During my A Levels, I got a letter from my sister saying that my mum had not just fell in a river, but that she had done it deliberately. When I got to school, Mr Parkinson asked me why I was late, and I just burst into tears. He sat me down in a little office and read the letter. He asked me about my family and I said that my sister had run away from home, and my dad was living with his girlfriend in London and had rented the rest of our house out. He then looked at me and said that I could come and live with him and his family, which I did.

I don't think I need to say anything more about Mr Parkinson. That single act says it all.

I eventually went to the University of York and after starting out doing Electronic Engineering (I had to pass Physics A Level in about 6 months at school to do this. I scraped an 'E'), I ended up with a BSc 2:1 Honours Degree in Computer Science instead. I hardly went to any lectures.

Instead I got the notes, and crammed for my exams, and did pretty well. I knew most of the stuff they were teaching anyway because I had taught it myself since I got my first computer in the early 80s, a ZX Spectrum 48k. I remember being fascinated by two things. George Boole and how his work unpacking the logic of language enabled the formation of Boolean Algebra (I later discovered he was a teacher's assistant in Doncaster! Ha! Imagine all the computers in the world based on the work of a guy who lived in Donny!), and something called the 'Turing machine'. I remember it blowing my mind and I felt touched by genius. I had no idea who Alan Turing was at the time. Cultural capital wasn't invented then.

After living in Leeds and opening the first, short lived internet cafe in Leeds City Centre (Planet Connect), I returned to Doncaster and immersed myself in my band, BRAZIL, named after my favourite film. I afforded to do this by making websites and programming stuff for local businesses. When my computer blew up, I decided I needed a night out with my best mate, Tom. I called for him round at his mum and dad's house, and his dad, Brian, answered the door. He asked me how things were going and I said rubbish, because I'd lost a load of work from my computer blowing up. Brian mentioned that our old school, Hatfield High, was looking for people. Maybe a technician, or even a teacher. I later handed my CV into the school and thought no more of it.

Apparently it was the last day of term when I got a phone call from Chris Coady, the Headteacher at Hatfield, asking me to come in for an interview. I told him I didn't have a suit, but he said to come in anyway. When I'd got to his office and sat down, his secretary came into the room. Chris said, "I'd like you to meet Gwyn. He's going to be working for us from September". I said, "what as?". He said, "a teacher of course."

I am now the CEO of seven schools, and doing what I believe I was born to do every day, through a series of weird events that were more likely not to have happened. I think it was inevitable, really.

I am now amazingly happy and living in Thorne, Doncaster with my wife, Kate and my two sons, Jac and Dylan, and Rufus the dog, in a beautiful house that we built with the help of our friend, Richard Wilson, master builder (Grand Designs, Season 13, Episode 1).

Jac and Dylan attend XP and XP East respectively.

I'm writing this book, not because of ego, but because it's incredibly important to share stories. Stories are who we are and what we learn from. When our stories go, we go. If I didn't share this story, who would know about the best teacher in the world?

Mr Brian Parkinson.

Andy's story

I was born in the back bedroom of a house in Hatfield, Doncaster in 1969. We only stayed there for a year and then we moved to a lovely, small semi-detached house in Wheatley Hills, just opposite Grove Park which was to become my playground throughout my childhood. I felt extremely privileged and extremely lucky.

However, in spite of our seemingly comfortable existence, we didn't have much money, my dad was a bricklayer (and a fine one at that) and my mum looked after me and my older brother, Mark. So things were tight. We didn't own a car, we didn't have a telephone and central heating was, to be honest, a concept of the future but we never went without and that was down to my mum and her ability to manage the little that we had to ensure this. We always got beautiful books at Christmas. We even managed to go on holiday twice before I was sixteen to Scarborough.

I went to Park Infant and then Park Junior school and I loved my time here. I loved reading and art as both of these would take me into other worlds. However, my main passion both at Junior School and then at Wheatley Middle school was football. To be honest I played every spare minute that I could up the playground 'hill' at Park School where one set of goalposts was set between a privet hedge and an oak tree (we weren't allowed on the grass!!) and then in the land locked playground of Wheatley Middle School (where we were only allowed to use a tennis ball and the nearest grass was about a quarter of a mile away!!). And during the holidays I spent nearly all of my time outdoors whether that was playing football or cricket or just out and about on my bike. I loved the park, I loved 'the field' in Wheatley, I loved the Town Fields and I loved Sandall Beat Wood. I explored all of these places with adventure and gusto. In addition, my passion for reading continued to grow and by the age of eleven I had read 'The Lord of the Rings' by Tolkien and had been irrevocably changed by reading 'To Kill a Mockingbird. As well as beginning to read more sophisticated literature, I also discovered a passion for American comics. I'd always read comics from an early age, predominantly Whizzer and Chips, The Beano and The Dandy, football comics like Roy of the Rovers and Score as well as dipping my toe into 2000AD, tempted by the Space Spinner free gift in issue # 1. In the late seventies and eighties I'd started to buy superhero comics like Spider-man so I could have a go at drawing the characters and very quickly was hooked on the stories. There was a certain exoticism to buying colour printed comics that came from the USA and I fell for it. These were starting to be comics that addressed more mature themes like death and loss and I relentlessly pursued Frank Miller's Daredevil (a superhero that got beat up a lot!) and John Byrne's Fantastic Four.

A large part of my childhood was spent at my maternal Grandma's in Edlington. She was on her own as my Grandad had left the family and lived away because of illness and we loved to spend time with her. She was an incredible woman. Full of kindness and intelligence unrealised by her place in society, she loved reading too. We devoured television on a Saturday night; inane but entertaining game shows such as 3-2-1 and Sale of the Century; British Police dramas like The Professionals and The Gentle Touch; US imports such as Hawaii Five-O, Starsky and Hutch, The Six Million Dollar Man etc etc... she loved to read too. It was here that I was allowed to stay up late and I first watched the first horror films where monsters emerged from Black Lagoons, ancient Egyptian mummies hounded profligate western grave robbers and Lon Chaney howled at the moon.

We also watched the full range of hammer horror films where Peter Cushing battled Christopher Lee, although my Grandma would leave us if it was Dracula - that was the only thing she was scared of and I mean the only thing. Spending so much time in a mining community had a profound effect on me and shaped my political thinking.

The air was thicker in Edlington, heavy with the smoke belching from the pit houses. It always seemed to be foggy in winter and I saw real hardship and poverty. I spent so much time in the place that I signed and played for Edlington White Stars for a couple of seasons, I can remember it was a black and gold striped kit and my Grandma darned my black football socks with brown wool. The pit dominated the village and when I was fifteen I saw the picket lines and the appalling behaviour of the police at first hand. For nothing more than ideological reasons a community was destroyed - this changed me fundamentally as I realised that there was an inequity in the world that needed to be challenged and changed.

I moved from Wheatley Middle School into secondary education at Danum School which was still suffering from the hangover of being a grammar school. Even though some staff at Wheatley thought I was decidedly average. I did really well in my end of year exams and was one of the few students from Wheatley to gain a place in the top set. I even started to think I might be capable enough to go to university!

This was a million miles away from most of my friends at Junior School and I suppose this was the first time I felt different and that my destiny might lie beyond Doncaster – how wrong could I be! Danum School was a bit of a blur to be honest. I meandered through without drama and I managed to pass a few 'O' levels and I was allowed into the Sixth form to study 'A' Levels. I spent most of time bunking off lessons and reading voraciously. I had now moved onto reading Albert Camus, Andre Gide, Jean Paul Sartre and I was existentially sneering at the rest of the world. I also started to write angst-ridden poetry.

Three important things happened to me at Danum. Firstly, I realised that if I wanted to continue to study it would have to be about books. Secondly, through the influence of my older brother Mark (who is a real punk!) my eyes and ears were opened up to the music of rebellion, in particular Crass and the Dead Kennedys. Finally, and most importantly, I met Nicola, my future wife who along with my daughter Beth I love more than life itself. After my A levels I secured a place at the University of East Anglia, but returned after a week because I missed home. School, or my life for that matter, had not prepared me for such a culture shock. I spent the next year reading loads of books, signing on, labouring on building sites and reading loads of books. I was then ready to return and continue my studies and I did so at the University of Newcastle upon Tyne to study English Literature. I enjoyed my time in the North East and like for so

many others who study there, it became like a second home. In lots of ways it was like Donny, but further north and nearer the coast!

After I got my degree I had to decide what do with it. I was at a bit of a loss. Nicola had already resolved that she wanted to be a teacher so without a great deal of thought I did the same and applied for a teaching training course. It was the greatest accident of my life. When I first worked with young people I realised that not only was it something that I could become pretty good at, I enjoyed it as well. And so, by accident rather than design, I found myself in the greatest and most noble profession in the world.

And the rest is another story...

Thank you

To our wives and families – thank you.

To all our amazing staff. Thank you for your support and challenge. **You made this school.**

To our parents. We won't let you down. We will never stop working hard. And we will never forget the trust you have put in us.

To Dr Anna Switzer, who came from the Everglades to Donny and helped us get started. The work you did in those three months with me and Andy was the most impressive piece of work we have ever witnessed, and we do not know anyone else who could have done that. In the world.

And to our students. Thank you for being your wonderful selves.

(Oh yeah... and not forgetting Ricky Elderkin for designing this book!)

In memory of Tyler Webb. You will not be forgotten.

Book List

Rework Jason Fried and David Heinemeier Hansson

Business for Punks James Watt

Anything **2000AD** (especially if it's written by Pat Mills)

Daredevil Frank Miller
Issue #163 - where he fights the Hulk - now that is courage!

All **EL publications**, especially **Leaders of their own learning.**
If you only buy one book, you must buy this one.
And 'An Ethic of Excellence'. Yes, that's right.

Why fly this way? by Kathy Greeley[18]
This inspired out first ever expedition.

All links are on our website **www.xpschool.org/howwexp**

---

18 If Ron is Obi Ron Kenobi, then Kathy is Princess Leia.
Photo©2019 www.jamiebubb.com

PROVENANCE

(you've got to go there
to come back, right?)

The creation of XP seems to be a combination of lucky coincidences, or serendipity at least. But do you make your own luck?

For our planet to even exist, and have intelligent life, is the combination of millions of seemingly unlikely accidents, the chance of it happening is almost an impossible probability. Some scientists believe it was inevitable - it had to happen, because we exist.

So, on our flight back from Boston, having met Ron Berger and Scott Hartl (EL, Expeditionary Learning) for the first time, Andy and I decided that it would be a good idea to send our kids Outward Bound. I knew there was an OB centre in Aberdovey, Wales.

What I didn't know when we made that decision was that EL came out of a collaboration with Outward Bound US and Harvard.

Outward Bound US came from Outward Bound UK.

Kurt Hahn, a Jewish, German educator, came over to England in the 1930s to get away from Nazi Germany. He created the school, Gordonstoun, which focused on character growth. He met Lawrence Holt, a shipping businessman, where they came up with the idea of Outward Bound, a training course to build character and improve the survival chances of young seamen.

The first Outward Bound centre was built in Aberdovey, Wales in 1941. My wife's brother (Richie 'Rocket' Wyatt) worked and lived there, so we used to go to Aberdovey quite often. The guy who ran OB was called AJ (Andrew Jeffries). AJ had a sister called Susan. Susan was my dad's first girlfriend.

Our design principles have been adapted and adopted from High Tech High. They formed theirs from the New Urban High School project, in New England, USA. This was delivered by the Big Picture Learning company in 1998, including Elliot Washor, the co-founder, who Andy and I first met during a visit to the Innovation Unit in London.

The first BPL school in the UK was formed in Doncaster by the Local Authority and the Innovation Unit in 2019. BPL UK have recently asked me to be their CEO. I am going to say, yes.

So, where the heck is this going?

I've no idea. I have no vision.
I just want to do the right thing.

I know to move on, we need good people.

I need to convince you that you
can do the right thing, too.

And if we love our children, we must
do the right thing.

But it's hard.

It's complex.

It's not easy.

Some people will say it's too risky, but...

There is no risk.

The risk is carrying on doing what you are doing now.

That will destroy you.

You have no choice.

You have to do it.

You can do it, too.